Introduction

Welcome to the 1 Year Bible Study. This introduction will help you to better understand the purpose of this study and how you can use it in your Bible study or church. Whether you use this method or not is not important. Growing in God's Word and applying what you have learned is what is of most importance. We hope that this study will help you know more of who God is, how we can live a holy life that glorifies God, and how we can make His name known to all peoples and places across the world.

Purpose

There are two purposes of this study. The first purpose is to learn how to study and apply God's Word on our own. Many times, our Biblical knowledge is founded on a leader, teacher, or pastor, but we don't know how to study and apply God's Word in our own quiet times. Although we may hear biblical preaching at church, we struggle to study and understand God's Word when we are outside of the church. We sometimes believe that we must be highly educated or a "professional" to understand God's Word. This belief is incorrect as God desires for you to know His Word. This study will help you to have confidence that studying and understanding God's Word is something everyone can do. The second purpose is to provide a template/method for beginning a new church as the Bible study begins to grow. There are those who do not yet have a church in their area, so this study is formatted in a way that a person or group can learn how to start and lead a church service that is grounded in God's Word. Currently, this study is used in quiet times, small groups, Bible studies, discipleship studies, and as a beginning for new churches.

This study begins with the Gospel of John, as John said in John 20:31 that his book was *"written so that you may believe that Jesus is the Christ, the Son of God, and that by believing you may have life in his name."* Through the Gospel of John, we will discover who Jesus is and how we can have eternal life through Him alone. Beginning with the Gospel of John, this study covers the 4 Gospels and 5 Epistles (or letters). Approximately every 10 weeks, a new Gospel will begin, so there is no need to stop and restart from the beginning when a new person joins the group/church as you will cover the Gospel several times. As you read through the New Testament, each lesson will build upon the previous section, so no previous Bible knowledge will be necessary.

Bible Reading Plan

First, you will see the "Bible Reading Plan". This is both an overview of the "1 Year Bible Study" and a simple Bible reading guide which someone can use in their quiet time or in a discipleship group. Each section represents a week. For example, in week 1 you will read John 1-3. If you finish the passages early, read them again to make sure you are fully understanding the passages. Next you will notice a memory verse to memorize for the week. For example, in week 1 you will memorize John 3:16. Finally, there are suggested passages to study with a partner or in a small group. For example, in week 1 you would study John 1:1-3, 1:4-5, 1:10-14, 3:16-18, and 3:19-21. At the end of the reading plan, you will find the "Foundations" passages. This can be studied at any time. There are passages for 5 important topics, which are foundations for the Christian faith.

1 Year Bible Study

This study is used as a template for a new church or to be used in a small group setting. The leader(s) will use this as a guide to lead the church or group throughout the year. By the end of the year, the leader(s) should be able to continue using this method to continue studying other books of the Bible. Below, we will briefly explain each part of the study.

Vision. Here, we share with the group the purpose for why we are meeting. A sample statement is given.

Care. At the beginning of our time together, we take time to discuss with others about their week to see how we can pray for and encourage one another. This can be done in small groups or 1 on 1, depending on the setting.

Accountability. After praying for each other, we will briefly review last week's lesson and see if there were any questions from the lesson or from the Bible reading from the previous week. Again, this can be done 1 on 1 or in a small group. We also ask each other if we were able to follow through with the goals we shared the previous week (For example: Did we share with someone what we learned in the last lesson? Did we share the gospel? Did we read our Bible?). This will be a great time of praise and encouragement as we share about what God is doing around us and through us from the past week.

Worship. This time will look different in each setting. This is a time of song that glorifies God, maybe a time of sharing testimonies, and/or even a time of giving our tithes and offerings (if a church).

New Lesson Context. For each lesson, a very brief context is given to remind everyone of what was learned the past week and what is happening in the current passage.

New Lesson Reading and Questions. Specific passages are given to study. The important thing is to focus only on these passages and not passages that haven't been studied yet. It is also good to reflect back on any previous passages that you have studied as a group. This will help you focus on the context of the passages and to grow in knowledge together as a group. Also, there are 5 sample questions given to discuss. First, we should seek to discover the overall meaning of the passages, not just focusing on one single verse. Second, we should seek to find what we can learn about God the Father, the Son, and the Spirit. Third, we will see what the passages teach about people and our relationship with God and with others. Fourth, we should look in the passages to see if there are any clear commands for all believers or if there are examples given which we should follow. Finally, we will be able to understand how we can apply what we have learned to our own lives.

Review. It is helpful to ask this review question after your study. This review question will help to see if everyone understood the passages and also to make sure that everyone can share what they learned with someone else.

Summary. For each lesson, a 1-2 sentence summary is given. This is to make sure that the main point is understood by the group. Some groups choose to memorize this summary statement.

Memory Verse. Each lesson will have a verse to memorize for the week. This is a key passage from the lesson to help everyone remember what they learned. Some groups practice memorizing this passage together.

1 Year
Bible Study

P.R.A.Y.   Many people have never prayed before or know how to pray.   We use the "P.R.A.Y." model to help everyone understand how to pray. At first, the leader will want to model this before the group, but later allow others to pray in this way as well. In this time of prayer, the focus is having prayers that are based on what we have learned from the passages in this week's lesson. For example, we Praise God for what we learned from the passage, then we Repent to God for any sins He has revealed to us, then we Ask God to help or guide to us to do what He has showed us. The final part, "Y", reminds us that we must respond with "Yes" to God and do what He has revealed to us.

Lord's Supper. For those who will use this as a church service, this is a suggested time to take the Lord's Supper. Some people use this as a chance to respond to the lesson as we repent of sins and reflect on Christ before we take the Lord's Supper.

Set Goals.   It is best to have a time to challenge one another to apply what they have learned throughout the week. For example, we encourage one another to share the gospel and share what they have learned with at least one other person, especially an unbeliever, this week. Also, we challenge the group to read over the full passage of Scripture that we had just studied. Finally, in a small group setting, it is helpful for each person to make a commitment before the group of what they will seek to do in the upcoming week. Maybe God revealed something to them in the passage that they need to do. Maybe God has reminded them of a specific person that they need to share with. Or, maybe there is a decision or confession of sin that the person needs to share. Much fruit comes when we set goals and keep one another accountable in their walk with the Lord.

Foundations

The final 5 lessons are our "Foundation" lessons. These can be done at the end of the year or whenever they are necessary (such as when someone decides to follow Christ). These lessons are key lessons for a new believer or an unbeliever who is seeking the truth to understand the core beliefs of becoming and living as a Christian. The passages should be studied and discussed together. These lessons are very helpful when someone is ready to follow Christ and take believer's baptism to make sure they understand the decision they are making and what it means to be a follower of Christ.

Bible Doctrine

It is important that those in our group, and especially our church, know what we believe. Our doctrine determines how we view God and His Word. A sample and suggested doctrinal statement is found at the end of this booklet. It is recommended that these doctrines are eventually studied as a group/church to be grounded on the core beliefs of the Christian faith.

*If you have questions about this study or see corrections which need to be made, email us at the6cokes@gmail.com.

Bible Reading Plan

Mark & James

Mark 1-3 (1:5)
Mark 1:1-8
Mark 1:9-11
Mark 1:14-20
Mark 2:1-7
Mark 2:8-12

Mark 4-5 (4:20)
Mark 4:1-9
Mark 4:13-20

Mark 6-7 (7:6b-7)
Mark 7:1-5
Mark 7:6-8
Mark 7:9-13
Mark 7:14-16
Mark 7:17-23

Mark 8-9 (8:35)
Mark 8:27-30
Mark 8:31-33
Mark 8:34-38

Mark 10-12 (10:45)
Mark 10:17-22
Mark 10:23-31
Mark 10:32-34
Mark 10:35-45

Mark 13-16 (13:10)
Mark 13:1-8
Mark 13:9-13
Mark 13:14-23
Mark 13:24-27
Mark 13:28-31
Mark 13:32-37

James 1 (1:22)
James 1:2-4
James 1:13-15
James 1:16-18
James 1:19-25
James 1:26-27

James 2 (2:10)
James 2:1-9
James 2:10-13
James 2:14-19
James 2:20-26

James 3 (3:8)
James 3:1-6
James 3:7-12
James 3:13-18

James 4-5 (4:17)
James 4:1-6
James 4:7-10
James 4:11-12
James 4:13-17

Luke & Philippians

Luke 1-3 (2:10)
Luke 1:26-38
Luke 2:1-7
Luke 2:8-20

Luke 4-6 (4:43)
Luke 4:38-41
Luke 4:42-44
Luke 5:17-19
Luke 5:20-26
Luke 5:27-32

Luke 7-10 (9:23)
Luke 8:22-25
Luke 8:26-29
Luke 8:30-33
Luke 8:34-39
Luke 9:10-17
Luke 9:18-20

Luke 11-14 (13:5)
Luke 13:22-30
Luke 14:15-20
Luke 14:21-24

Luke 15-17 (15:10)
Luke 15:1-7
Luke 15:8-10
Luke 16:19-31

Luke 18-21 (19:10)
Luke 18:9-14
Luke 18:18-23
Luke 18:24-30
Luke 19:1-10

Luke 22-24 (24:46-47)
Luke 22:1-23
Luke 23:32-49
Luke 24

Philippians 1 (1:20)
Philippians 1:12-20   Philippians 1:27-30
Philippians 1:21-26

Philippians 2 (2:14-15)
Philippians 2:1-4   Philippians 2:9-11
Philippians 2:5-8   Philippians 2:12-18

Philippians 3 (3:10-11)
Philippians 3:7-11   Philippians 3:17-21
Philippians 3:12-16

Philippians 4 (4:8)
Philippians 4:6-7   Philippians 4:10-13
Philippians 4:8-9

John & 1 John

John 1-3 (3:16)
John 1:1-3
John 1:4-5
John 1:10-14
John 3:16-18
John 3:19-21

John 4-7 (4:14)
John 4:1-9
John 4:10-15
John 4:16-19
John 4:20-26
John 4:27-30; 39-42

John 8-10 (10:27-28)
John 10:1-6
John 10:7-10
John 10:11-18
John 10:19-30

John 11-13 (12:25-26)
John 12:9-19
John 12:20-28
John 12:29-36
John 12:37-43
John 12:44-50

John 14-17 (14:6)
John 14:1-6
John 14:7-14
John 14:15-26
John 15:26-27; 16:1-15

John 18-19 (18:37b)
John 18:1-12
John 18:28-38
John 19:1-42

John 20-21 (20:31)
John 20:1-18
John 20:30-31
John 21:24-25

1 John 1-2 (1:9)
1 John 1:1-4   1 John 2:3-6
1 John 1:5-2:2   1 John 2:7-11
   1 John 2:15-17

1 John 3 (3:16)
1 John 3:1-6   1 John 3:18-22
1 John 3:7-10   1 John 3:23-24
1 John 3:16-17

1 John 4-5 (4:10)
1 John 4:1-6   1 John 4:13-19
1 John 4:7-12   1 John 4:20-5:5

Foundations

Salvation
John 1:11-13
John 3:1-21
John 11:25-26
Romans 3:23
Romans 6:6-10
Romans 6:23
Romans 10:9-13
2 Corinthians 5:17
Ephesians 2:1-10
1 John 1:5-2:2

Following Jesus
Matthew 7:13-14
Mark 8:34-38
John 14:6
Acts 4:12
2 Corinthians 5:15
1 Timothy 2:5-6

Baptism
Matthew 28:16-20
Acts 2:37-42
Acts 8:26-39
Acts 16:25-34
Romans 6:1-11

Telling Others
Matthew 5:13-16
Matthew 28:16-20
Mark 5:18-20
John 4:25-30, 39-42
Romans 1:16
Romans 10:8-15
2 Corinthians 4:1-6
2 Timothy 2:2
1 Peter 3:13-17

Church
Matthew 26:26-30
Acts 2:37-47
1 Corinthians 11:17-32
1 Timothy 3:1-13
Titus 1:5-9; 2:1-8

Romans

Romans 1 (Romans 1:20)
Romans 1:16-17
Romans 1:18-20
Romans 1:21-25
Romans 1:26-32

Romans 2-3 (Romans 3:23)
Romans 3:9-23
Romans 3:20-22
Romans 3:23-27

Romans 4-5 (Romans 5:1)
Romans 4:1-5
Romans 5:1-5
Romans 6:1-11

Romans 6-7 (Romans 6:23)
Romans 6:1-14
Romans 7:18-25

Romans 8-11 (Romans 8:1)
Romans 8:1-2
Romans 8:3-11
Romans 8:12-17
Romans 8:26-27

Romans 12-14 (Romans 12:1-2)
Romans 12:1-2
Romans 12:3-8
Romans 12:9-15
Romans 12:16-21

Romans 15-16 (Romans 15:20)
Romans 15:14-17
Romans 15:18-24
Romans 16:25-27

Matt. & Ephesians

Focus: Sermon on the Mt & Olivet Discourse

Matt. 1-4 (5:16)
Matthew 5:21-26
Matthew 5:27-32
Matthew 5:33-37
Matthew 5:38-48

Matt. 8-11 (6:1)
Matthew 6:1-4
Matthew 6:5-15
Matthew 6:16-18

Matt. 12-14 (6:33)
Matthew 6:19-24
Matthew 6:25-34

Matt. 15-18 (7:14)
Matthew 7:13-23
Matthew 7:24-29

Matt. 19-22 (24:14)
Matthew 24:1-14
Matthew 24:23-28
Matthew 24:36-44
Matthew 24:45-51

Matt. 23-25 (25:13)
Matthew 25:1-13
Matthew 25:31-46

Matt. 26-28 (28:18-20)
Matthew 27:57-66
Matthew 28:1-10
Matthew 28:11-15
Matthew 28:16-20

Ephesians 1-2 (2:8-9)
Ephesians 1:20-23
Ephesians 2:1-10

Ephesians 3 (3:20)
Ephesians 3:14-19
Ephesians 3:20-21

Ephesians 4 (4:1-3)
Ephesians 4:1-6
Ephesians 4:15-16
Ephesians 4:25-5:2
Ephesians 5:3-5:5

Ephesians 5 (5:15-16)
Ephesians 5:22-33
Ephesians 6:1-4
Ephesians 6:5-9

Ephesians 6 (6:11)
Ephesians 6:1-13
Ephesians 6:14-18
Ephesians 6:19-20

Gospel of John

Passage: John 1-3

Vision: "We are a community of baptized believers and seekers of the truth meeting regularly to obey the commands of Scripture and making God's glory known to all peoples." Habakkuk 2:14

Care: How are you doing? Prayer for one another.

Accountability: Review last week's lesson and goals. Did you share with someone?

Worship (song, testimony, tithes/offerings, etc)

New Lesson Context: John was a close follower of Jesus who wrote about Jesus and what Jesus said. He began his book by calling Jesus, "The Word". One reason is because the Old Testament is God's Word and it all points to Jesus. Further, Jesus reveals to us who God is. John also explained the relationship between Jesus and God. We will discover what that relationship is in verse 1.
**Before starting the book of John, it is helpful to give a summary of the Old Testament or a Creation to Christ presentation.

New Lesson Reading & Questions:
*Passages to study: John 1:1-5, 10-14; 3:16-18, 19–21
Questions to discover:
1. In context, summarize this passage as a whole?
2. What do we learn about God/Jesus/Holy Spirit?
3. What do we learn about people?
4. Are there any commands to obey or examples to follow?
5. What are ways I can apply what I have learned in my life?

Review: How would you share this lesson with someone who was not here today?

Summary: Jesus is God. If I want to be a child of God and have eternal life, I must accept, believe, and follow Jesus.

Memory Verse: John 3:16

P.R.A.Y. (Praise, Repent, Ask, and say "Yes" to what God has revealed to you)

Lord's Supper (if you are a church)

Set Goals:
1. Share the gospel and what you learned this week
2. Read John 1-3
3. Share with group how you will respond to the lesson this week

Passage: John 4-7

Vision: "We are a community of baptized believers and seekers of the truth meeting regularly to obey the commands of Scripture and making God's glory known to all peoples." Habakkuk 2:14

Care: How are you doing? Prayer for one another.

Accountability: Review last week's lesson and goals. Did you share with someone?

Worship (song, testimony, tithes/offerings, etc)

New Lesson Context: We have learned that Jesus is God. We also learned that God loves us by giving eternal life to those who accept Jesus, repent of their sins, and follow Jesus. In today's lesson, Jesus will show His love for all people as He traveled through a city called Samaria. The Jewish people did not like the Samaritan people, but Jesus went there anyway.

New Lesson Reading & Questions:
*Passages to study: John 4:1-9, 10-15, 16-19, 20-26, 27-30, 39-42
Questions to discover:
1. In context, summarize this passage as a whole?
2. What do we learn about God/Jesus/Holy Spirit?
3. What do we learn about people?
4. Are there any commands to obey or examples to follow?
5. What are ways I can apply what I have learned in my life?

Review: How would you share this lesson with someone who was not here today?

Summary: Jesus is the Promised Messiah and the Savior of the World. Those who know Jesus share the Good News with others.

Memory Verse: John 4:14

P.R.A.Y. (Praise, Repent, Ask, and say "Yes" to what God has revealed to you)

Lord's Supper (if you are a church)

Set Goals:
1. Share the gospel and what you learned this week
2. Read John 4-7
3. Share with group how you will respond to the lesson this week

Passage: John 8-10

Vision: "We are a community of baptized believers and seekers of the truth meeting regularly to obey the commands of Scripture and making God's glory known to all peoples." Habakkuk 2:14

Care: How are you doing? Prayer for one another.

Accountability: Review last week's lesson and goals. Did you share with someone?

Worship (song, testimony, tithes/offerings, etc)

New Lesson Context: Jesus did many miracles to prove He was the Messiah. After healing a blind man, Jesus used an illustration of a shepherd and sheep to explain His relationship with those who follow Him.

New Lesson Reading & Questions:
> *Passages to study: John 10:1-6, 7-10, 11-18, 19-30
> Questions to discover:
>> 1. In context, summarize this passage as a whole?
>> 2. What do we learn about God/Jesus/Holy Spirit?
>> 3. What do we learn about people?
>> 4. Are there any commands to obey or examples to follow?
>> 5. What are ways I can apply what I have learned in my life?

Review: How would you share this lesson with someone who was not here today?

Summary: We are like lost sheep who need a shepherd. Jesus is our Great Shepherd who is willing to die for His sheep.

Memory Verse: John 10:27-28

P.R.A.Y. (Praise, Repent, Ask, and say "Yes" to what God has revealed to you)

Lord's Supper (if you are a church)

Set Goals:
> 1. Share the gospel and what you learned this week
> 2. Read John 8-10
> 3. Share with group how you will respond to the lesson this week

Passage: John 11-13

Vision: "We are a community of baptized believers and seekers of the truth meeting regularly to obey the commands of Scripture and making God's glory known to all peoples." Habakkuk 2:14

Care: How are you doing? Prayer for one another.

Accountability: Review last week's lesson and goals. Did you share with someone?

Worship (song, testimony, tithes/offerings, etc)

New Lesson Context: Jesus raised a dead man, named Lazarus, from the dead. After this, many crowds followed Jesus to see more miracles. Jesus then entered into Jerusalem on a donkey, which fulfilled a prophecy about the Messiah from Zechariah 9:9.

New Lesson Reading & Questions:
> *Passages to study: John 12:9-19, 20-28, 29-36, 37-43, 44-50
> Questions to discover:
>> 1. In context, summarize this passage as a whole?
>> 2. What do we learn about God/Jesus/Holy Spirit?
>> 3. What do we learn about people?
>> 4. Are there any commands to obey or examples to follow?
>> 5. What are ways I can apply what I have learned in my life?

Review: How would you share this lesson with someone who was not here today?

Summary: A true believer loves the praise of God more than the praise of man. They follow Jesus even through persecution.

Memory Verse: John 12:25-26

P.R.A.Y. (Praise, Repent, Ask, and say "Yes" to what God has revealed to you)

Lord's Supper (if you are a church)

Set Goals:
> 1. Share the gospel and what you learned this week
> 2. Read John 11-13
> 3. Share with group how you will respond to the lesson this week

Passage: John 14-17

Vision: "We are a community of baptized believers and seekers of the truth meeting regularly to obey the commands of Scripture and making God's glory known to all peoples." Habakkuk 2:14

Care: How are you doing? Prayer for one another.

Accountability: Review last week's lesson and goals. Did you share with someone?

Worship (song, testimony, tithes/offerings, etc)

New Lesson Context: After Jesus entered Jerusalem, He knew that His death was coming soon. Jesus then began to prepare His disciples by prophesying about His death, but also giving them comfort that He would not leave them alone. Finally, Jesus reminded them again that God is 3 persons in 1 (God the Father, God the Son, and God the Spirit).

New Lesson Reading & Questions:
>   *Passages to study: John 14:1-6, 7-14, 15-26; 15:26-27; 16:1-15
>   Questions to discover:
>>   1. In context, summarize this passage as a whole?
>>   2. What do we learn about God/Jesus/Holy Spirit?
>>   3. What do we learn about people?
>>   4. Are there any commands to obey or examples to follow?
>>   5. What are ways I can apply what I have learned in my life?

Review: How would you share this lesson with someone who was not here today?

Summary: Jesus prophesied His death, but He promised that He would give Believers His Spirit to guide us.

Memory Verse: John 14:6

P.R.A.Y. (Praise, Repent, Ask, and say "Yes" to what God has revealed to you)

Lord's Supper (if you are a church)

Set Goals:
>   1. Share the gospel and what you learned this week
>   2. Read John 14-17
>   3. Share with group how you will respond to the lesson this week

Passage: John 18-19

**If needed, this lesson and the next lesson can be combined if there is time.
Vision: "We are a community of baptized believers and seekers of the truth meeting regularly to obey the commands of Scripture and making God's glory known to all peoples." Habakkuk 2:14

Care: How are you doing? Prayer for one another.

Accountability: Review last week's lesson and goals. Did you share with someone?

Worship (song, testimony, tithes/offerings, etc)

New Lesson Context: Many of the religious leaders were jealous of Jesus, so they planned to convince the leaders of Rome to have Jesus killed. They knew that if Jesus was dead, then He could not be the Messiah or God.

New Lesson Reading & Questions:
>   *Passages to study: John 18:1-12, 28-38; 19:1-42
>   Questions to discover:
>>   1. In context, summarize this passage as a whole?
>>   2. What do we learn about God/Jesus/Holy Spirit?
>>   3. What do we learn about people?
>>   4. Are there any commands to obey or examples to follow?
>>   5. What are ways I can apply what I have learned in my life?

Review: How would you share this lesson with someone who was not here today?

Summary: Jesus was sinless, but He willingly allowed himself to be arrested and killed on a cross. This is the punishment I deserve for my sins.

Memory Verse: John 18:37b

P.R.A.Y. (Praise, Repent, Ask, and say "Yes" to what God has revealed to you)

Lord's Supper (if you are a church)

Set Goals:
>   1. Share the gospel and what you learned this week
>   2. Read John 18-19
>   3. Share with group how you will respond to the lesson this week

Passage: John 20-21

Vision: "We are a community of baptized believers and seekers of the truth meeting regularly to obey the commands of Scripture and making God's glory known to all peoples." Habakkuk 2:14

Care: How are you doing? Prayer for one another.

Accountability: Review last week's lesson and goals. Did you share with someone?

Worship (song, testimony, tithes/offerings, etc)

New Lesson Context: Jesus died on a cross and many thought the Messiah was dead. He was buried in a tomb on Friday and on Sunday Mary Magdalene came to the tomb.

New Lesson Reading & Questions:
>*Passages to study: John 20:1-18, 30-31; 21:24-25
>Questions to discover:
>>1. In context, summarize this passage as a whole?
>>2. What do we learn about God/Jesus/Holy Spirit?
>>3. What do we learn about people?
>>4. Are there any commands to obey or examples to follow?
>>5. What are ways I can apply what I have learned in my life?

Review: How would you share this lesson with someone who was not here today?

Summary: Jesus proved He was fully God and the Messiah by raising from the dead!

Memory Verse: John 20:31

P.R.A.Y. (Praise, Repent, Ask, and say "Yes" to what God has revealed to you)

Lord's Supper (if you are a church)

Set Goals:
>1. Share the gospel and what you learned this week
>2. Read John 20-21
>3. Share with group how you will respond to the lesson this week

1 John

Passage: 1 John 1-2

Vision: "We are a community of baptized believers and seekers of the truth meeting regularly to obey the commands of Scripture and making God's glory known to all peoples." Habakkuk 2:14

Care: How are you doing? Prayer for one another.

Accountability: Review last week's lesson and goals. Did you share with someone?

Worship (song, testimony, tithes/offerings, etc)

New Lesson Context: John wrote the Gospel of John to tell the true story of Jesus. He then continued to write letters to churches to teach them how to follow Jesus. The book of 1 John is one of those letters.

New Lesson Reading & Questions:
*Passages to study: 1 John 1:1-4; 1:5-2:2; 2:3-11, 15-17
Questions to discover:
1. In context, summarize this passage as a whole?
2. What do we learn about God/Jesus/Holy Spirit?
3. What do we learn about people?
4. Are there any commands to obey or examples to follow?
5. What are ways I can apply what I have learned in my life?

Review: How would you share this lesson with someone who was not here today?

Summary: A child of God walks in the light like Jesus walked. We must confess our sins and not love the things of the world.

Memory Verse: 1 John 1:9

P.R.A.Y. (Praise, Repent, Ask, and say "Yes" to what God has revealed to you)

Lord's Supper (if you are a church)

Set Goals:
1. Share the gospel and what you learned this week
2. Read 1 John 1-2
3. Share with group how you will respond to the lesson this week

Passage: 1 John 3

Vision: "We are a community of baptized believers and seekers of the truth meeting regularly to obey the commands of Scripture and making God's glory known to all peoples." Habakkuk 2:14

Care: How are you doing? Prayer for one another.

Accountability: Review last week's lesson and goals. Did you share with someone?

Worship (song, testimony, tithes/offerings, etc)

New Lesson Context: John wrote the Gospel of John to tell the true story of Jesus. He then continued to write letters to churches to teach them how to follow Jesus. The book of 1 John is one of those letters.

New Lesson Reading & Questions:
> *Passages to study: 1 John 3:1-6, 7-10, 16-17, 18-22, 23-24
> Questions to discover:
> > 1. In context, summarize this passage as a whole?
> > 2. What do we learn about God/Jesus/Holy Spirit?
> > 3. What do we learn about people?
> > 4. Are there any commands to obey or examples to follow?
> > 5. What are ways I can apply what I have learned in my life?

Review: How would you share this lesson with someone who was not here today?

Summary: A child of God loves like Jesus loved. This proves that God's Spirit is in us.

Memory Verse: 1 John 3:16

P.R.A.Y. (Praise, Repent, Ask, and say "Yes" to what God has revealed to you)

Lord's Supper (if you are a church)

Set Goals:
> 1. Share the gospel and what you learned this week
> 2. Read 1 John 3
> 3. Share with group how you will respond to the lesson this week

Passage: 1 John 4-5

Vision: "We are a community of baptized believers and seekers of the truth meeting regularly to obey the commands of Scripture and making God's glory known to all peoples." Habakkuk 2:14

Care: How are you doing? Prayer for one another.

Accountability: Review last week's lesson and goals. Did you share with someone?

Worship (song, testimony, tithes/offerings, etc)

New Lesson Context: John wrote the Gospel of John to tell the true story of Jesus. He then continued to write letters to churches to teach them how to follow Jesus. The book of 1 John is one of those letters.

New Lesson Reading & Questions:
>   *Passages to study: 1 John 4:1-6, 7-12, 13-19; 4:20-5:5
>   Questions to discover:
>>   1. In context, summarize this passage as a whole?
>>   2. What do we learn about God/Jesus/Holy Spirit?
>>   3. What do we learn about people?
>>   4. Are there any commands to obey or examples to follow?
>>   5. What are ways I can apply what I have learned in my life?

Review: How would you share this lesson with someone who was not here today?

Summary: We can love because God first loved us and God has given us His Spirit.

Memory Verse: 1 John 4:10

P.R.A.Y. (Praise, Repent, Ask, and say "Yes" to what God has revealed to you)

Lord's Supper (if you are a church)

Set Goals:
>   1. Share the gospel and what you learned this week
>   2. Read 1 John 4-5
>   3. Share with group how you will respond to the lesson this week

Gospel of Luke

Passage: Luke 1-3

Vision: "We are a community of baptized believers and seekers of the truth meeting regularly to obey the commands of Scripture and making God's glory known to all peoples." Habakkuk 2:14

Care: How are you doing? Prayer for one another.

Accountability: Review last week's lesson and goals. Did you share with someone?

Worship (song, testimony, tithes/offerings, etc)

New Lesson Context: For 2,000 years, people were waiting for the promised Messiah to save them from their sins. The Gospel of Luke is a detailed account/story of the Messiah's birth, life, death, and resurrection.

New Lesson Reading & Questions:
> *Passages to study: Luke 1:26-38; 2:1-7, 8-20
> Questions to discover:
>> 1. In context, summarize this passage as a whole?
>> 2. What do we learn about God/Jesus/Holy Spirit?
>> 3. What do we learn about people?
>> 4. Are there any commands to obey or examples to follow?
>> 5. What are ways I can apply what I have learned in my life?

Review: How would you share this lesson with someone who was not here today?

Summary: Jesus is the promised Messiah, Son of God, and Savior of the World.

Memory Verse: Luke 2:10

P.R.A.Y. (Praise, Repent, Ask, and say "Yes" to what God has revealed to you)

Lord's Supper (if you are a church)

Set Goals:
> 1. Share the gospel and what you learned this week
> 2. Read Luke 1-3
> 3. Share with group how you will respond to the lesson this week

Passage: Luke 4-6

Vision: "We are a community of baptized believers and seekers of the truth meeting regularly to obey the commands of Scripture and making God's glory known to all peoples." Habakkuk 2:14

Care: How are you doing? Prayer for one another.

Accountability: Review last week's lesson and goals. Did you share with someone?

Worship (song, testimony, tithes/offerings, etc)

New Lesson Context: Previously, Luke wrote about Jesus' birth. Then, Luke wrote about Jesus' baptism. After this, Satan tried to tempt Jesus and the people of Jesus' hometown drove Him out of that town. But, this did not stop Jesus from doing what He came to the earth to do. (Luke 4:43 and 5:32)

New Lesson Reading & Questions:
>*Passages to study: Luke 4:38-41, 42-44; 5:17-19, 20-26, 27-32
>Questions to discover:
>>1. In context, summarize this passage as a whole?
>>2. What do we learn about God/Jesus/Holy Spirit?
>>3. What do we learn about people?
>>4. Are there any commands to obey or examples to follow?
>>5. What are ways I can apply what I have learned in my life?

Review: How would you share this lesson with someone who was not here today?

Summary: Jesus is more powerful than sickness and demons, but His greatest power is the ability to forgive sins.

Memory Verse: Luke 4:43

P.R.A.Y. (Praise, Repent, Ask, and say "Yes" to what God has revealed to you)

Lord's Supper (if you are a church)

Set Goals:
>1. Share the gospel and what you learned this week
>2. Read Luke 4-6
>3. Share with group how you will respond to the lesson this week

Passage: Luke 7-10

Vision: "We are a community of baptized believers and seekers of the truth meeting regularly to obey the commands of Scripture and making God's glory known to all peoples." Habakkuk 2:14

Care: How are you doing? Prayer for one another.

Accountability: Review last week's lesson and goals. Did you share with someone?

Worship (song, testimony, tithes/offerings, etc)

New Lesson Context: Jesus continued to show His power and to teach people about the Kingdom of God. He then began to send out His 12 closest followers, called disciples, to continue this message across Israel.

New Lesson Reading & Questions:
> *Passages to study: Luke 8:22-25, 26-29, 30-33, 34-39; 9:10-17, 18-20
> Questions to discover:
>> 1. In context, summarize this passage as a whole?
>> 2. What do we learn about God/Jesus/Holy Spirit?
>> 3. What do we learn about people?
>> 4. Are there any commands to obey or examples to follow?
>> 5. What are ways I can apply what I have learned in my life?

Review: How would you share this lesson with someone who was not here today?

Summary: After seeing Jesus having power over nature, demons, and even people's needs, Peter confesses that Jesus is the Messiah.

Memory Verse: Luke 9:23

P.R.A.Y. (Praise, Repent, Ask, and say "Yes" to what God has revealed to you)

Lord's Supper (if you are a church)

Set Goals:
> 1. Share the gospel and what you learned this week
> 2. Read Luke 7-10
> 3. Share with group how you will respond to the lesson this week

Passage: Luke 11-14

Vision: "We are a community of baptized believers and seekers of the truth meeting regularly to obey the commands of Scripture and making God's glory known to all peoples." Habakkuk 2:14

Care: How are you doing? Prayer for one another.

Accountability: Review last week's lesson and goals. Did you share with someone?

Worship (song, testimony, tithes/offerings, etc)

New Lesson Context: Jesus continued teaching about the Kingdom of God. He urged the people to repent and follow God. He also warned them about loving the things of the world more than the things of God. (Luke 12:34)

New Lesson Reading & Questions:
> *Passages to study: Luke 13:22-30; 14:15-20, 21-24
> Questions to discover:
>> 1. In context, summarize this passage as a whole?
>> 2. What do we learn about God/Jesus/Holy Spirit?
>> 3. What do we learn about people?
>> 4. Are there any commands to obey or examples to follow?
>> 5. What are ways I can apply what I have learned in my life?

Review: How would you share this lesson with someone who was not here today?

Summary: We must not make excuses to not follow Jesus. We must choose to follow Jesus today.

Memory Verse: Luke 13:5

P.R.A.Y. (Praise, Repent, Ask, and say "Yes" to what God has revealed to you)

Lord's Supper (if you are a church)

Set Goals:
> 1. Share the gospel and what you learned this week
> 2. Read Luke 11-14
> 3. Share with group how you will respond to the lesson this week

Passage: Luke 15-17

Vision: "We are a community of baptized believers and seekers of the truth meeting regularly to obey the commands of Scripture and making God's glory known to all peoples." Habakkuk 2:14

Care: How are you doing? Prayer for one another.

Accountability: Review last week's lesson and goals. Did you share with someone?

Worship (song, testimony, tithes/offerings, etc)

New Lesson Context: Following God is difficult. We cannot choose to follow both the world and God. After this life, we will spend eternity with God or apart from God. Jesus is our Shepherd and He rejoices when His sheep choose to follow and obey Him.

New Lesson Reading & Questions:
   *Passages to study: Luke 15:1-7, 8-10; 16:19-31
   Questions to discover:
      1. In context, summarize this passage as a whole?
      2. What do we learn about God/Jesus/Holy Spirit?
      3. What do we learn about people?
      4. Are there any commands to obey or examples to follow?
      5. What are ways I can apply what I have learned in my life?

Review: How would you share this lesson with someone who was not here today?

Summary: Those who reject Jesus will spend eternity being tormented in Hell away from God.

Memory Verse: Luke 15:10

P.R.A.Y. (Praise, Repent, Ask, and say "Yes" to what God has revealed to you)

Lord's Supper (if you are a church)

Set Goals:
      1. Share the gospel and what you learned this week
      2. Read Luke 15-17
      3. Share with group how you will respond to the lesson this week

Passage: Luke 18-21

Vision: "We are a community of baptized believers and seekers of the truth meeting regularly to obey the commands of Scripture and making God's glory known to all peoples." Habakkuk 2:14

Care: How are you doing? Prayer for one another.

Accountability: Review last week's lesson and goals. Did you share with someone?

Worship (song, testimony, tithes/offerings, etc)

New Lesson Context: In chapters 18-19, Jesus talked about two types of people and talked about which of them will enter the Kingdom of God. First, there was a rich young ruler and a Pharisee who followed the religious laws and had many possessions. Second, there were those who were looked down upon in their society (tax collectors, widows, and children).

New Lesson Reading & Questions:
*Passages to study: Luke 18:9-14, 18-23, 24-30; 19:1-10
Questions to discover:
1. In context, summarize this passage as a whole?
2. What do we learn about God/Jesus/Holy Spirit?
3. What do we learn about people?
4. Are there any commands to obey or examples to follow?
5. What are ways I can apply what I have learned in my life?

Review: How would you share this lesson with someone who was not here today?

Summary: Our worldly possessions and and sins keep us from the Kingdom of God, but God saves those who repent and follow Christ alone.

Memory Verse: Luke 19:10

P.R.A.Y. (Praise, Repent, Ask, and say "Yes" to what God has revealed to you)

Lord's Supper (if you are a church)

Set Goals:
1. Share the gospel and what you learned this week
2. Read Luke 18-21
3. Share with group how you will respond to the lesson this week

Passage: Luke 22-24

*This is a long passage. Chapters 22-23 can be summarized if needed, then focus on 24.

Vision: "We are a community of baptized believers and seekers of the truth meeting regularly to obey the commands of Scripture and making God's glory known to all peoples." Habakkuk 2:14

Care: How are you doing? Prayer for one another.

Accountability: Review last week's lesson and goals. Did you share with someone?

Worship (song, testimony, tithes/offerings, etc)

New Lesson Context: Many religious leaders became jealous of Jesus. Also, one of Jesus' disciples became a traitor who would lead the police to arrest Jesus. In chapter 22, Jesus knew He was about to be arrested, so He celebrated the Passover meal with His disciples, knowing it would be His final meal with them. He then was arrested, beaten, and killed on a cross.

New Lesson Reading & Questions:
    *Passages to study: Luke 22:1-23; 23:32-49; 24:1-53
    Questions to discover:
        1. In context, summarize this passage as a whole?
        2. What do we learn about God/Jesus/Holy Spirit?
        3. What do we learn about people?
        4. Are there any commands to obey or examples to follow?
        5. What are ways I can apply what I have learned in my life?

Review: How would you share this lesson with someone who was not here today?

Summary: Jesus is the promised Messiah who fulfilled the prophecies that He would suffer, die, raise from the dead and offer forgiveness of sins to the nations.

Memory Verse: Luke 24:46-47

P.R.A.Y. (Praise, Repent, Ask, and say "Yes" to what God has revealed to you)

Lord's Supper (if you are a church)

Set Goals:
    1. Share the gospel and what you learned this week
    2. Read Luke 22-24
    3. Share with group how you will respond to the lesson this week

Philippians

Passage: Philippians 1

Vision: "We are a community of baptized believers and seekers of the truth meeting regularly to obey the commands of Scripture and making God's glory known to all peoples." Habakkuk 2:14

Care: How are you doing? Prayer for one another.

Accountability: Review last week's lesson and goals. Did you share with someone?

Worship (song, testimony, tithes/offerings, etc)

New Lesson Context: Paul was a follower of Jesus who started many churches. He wrote letters to those churches, reminding them about how to follow Jesus and be a healthy church. Philippians was written to a church in Philippi. He began his letter reminding them about when he was put in prison the last time he was in Philippi. (Acts 16)

New Lesson Reading & Questions:
>   *Passages to study: Philippians 1:12-20; 21-26; 27-30
>   Questions to discover:
>> 1. In context, summarize this passage as a whole?
>> 2. What do we learn about God/Jesus/Holy Spirit?
>> 3. What do we learn about people?
>> 4. Are there any commands to obey or examples to follow?
>> 5. What are ways I can apply what I have learned in my life?

Review: How would you share this lesson with someone who was not here today?

Summary: In all situations, I must live worthy of the gospel, looking for opportunities to share the gospel with others.

Memory Verse: Philippians 1:20

P.R.A.Y. (Praise, Repent, Ask, and say "Yes" to what God has revealed to you)

Lord's Supper (if you are a church)

Set Goals:
>> 1. Share the gospel and what you learned this week
>> 2. Read Philippians 1
>> 3. Share with group how you will respond to the lesson this week

Passage: Philippians 2

Vision: "We are a community of baptized believers and seekers of the truth meeting regularly to obey the commands of Scripture and making God's glory known to all peoples." Habakkuk 2:14

Care: How are you doing? Prayer for one another.

Accountability: Review last week's lesson and goals. Did you share with someone?

Worship (song, testimony, tithes/offerings, etc)

New Lesson Context: After Paul wrote about his desire to spread the gospel in all situations, he then encouraged the church in Philippi to be united through humility.

New Lesson Reading & Questions:
>*Passages to study: Philippians 2:1-4, 5-8, 9-11, 12-18
>Questions to discover:
>>1. In context, summarize this passage as a whole?
>>2. What do we learn about God/Jesus/Holy Spirit?
>>3. What do we learn about people?
>>4. Are there any commands to obey or examples to follow?
>>5. What are ways I can apply what I have learned in my life?

Review: How would you share this lesson with someone who was not here today?

Summary: I must be humble and put other people first, like Jesus did, to be an example of Jesus to the world.

Memory Verse: Philippians 2:14-15

P.R.A.Y. (Praise, Repent, Ask, and say "Yes" to what God has revealed to you)

Lord's Supper (if you are a church)

Set Goals:
>1. Share the gospel and what you learned this week
>2. Read Philippians 2
>3. Share with group how you will respond to the lesson this week

Passage: Philippians 3

Vision: "We are a community of baptized believers and seekers of the truth meeting regularly to obey the commands of Scripture and making God's glory known to all peoples." Habakkuk 2:14

Care: How are you doing? Prayer for one another.

Accountability: Review last week's lesson and goals. Did you share with someone?

Worship (song, testimony, tithes/offerings, etc)

New Lesson Context: In chapter 1, Paul wrote of the importance of sharing the gospel. In chapter 2, Paul said that we must live the Christian life in humility. In chapter 3, Paul wrote that many people are prideful about their good deeds.

New Lesson Reading & Questions:
> *Passages to study: Philippians 3:7-11, 12-16, 17-21
> Questions to discover:
>> 1. In context, summarize this passage as a whole?
>> 2. What do we learn about God/Jesus/Holy Spirit?
>> 3. What do we learn about people?
>> 4. Are there any commands to obey or examples to follow?
>> 5. What are ways I can apply what I have learned in my life?

Review: How would you share this lesson with someone who was not here today?

Summary: Everything in this world is worthless compared to following Jesus.

Memory Verse: Philippians 3:10-11

P.R.A.Y. (Praise, Repent, Ask, and say "Yes" to what God has revealed to you)

Lord's Supper (if you are a church)

Set Goals:
> 1. Share the gospel and what you learned this week
> 2. Read Philippians 3
> 3. Share with group how you will respond to the lesson this week

Passage: Philippians 4

Vision: "We are a community of baptized believers and seekers of the truth meeting regularly to obey the commands of Scripture and making God's glory known to all peoples." Habakkuk 2:14

Care: How are you doing? Prayer for one another.

Accountability: Review last week's lesson and goals. Did you share with someone?

Worship (song, testimony, tithes/offerings, etc)

New Lesson Context: Paul ended his letter with a final reminder for the church to continue to be a healthy church, share the Gospel, and spread God's glory to all nations.

New Lesson Reading & Questions:
> *Passages to study: Philippians 4:6-7, 8-9, 10-13
> Questions to discover:
>> 1. In context, summarize this passage as a whole?
>> 2. What do we learn about God/Jesus/Holy Spirit?
>> 3. What do we learn about people?
>> 4. Are there any commands to obey or examples to follow?
>> 5. What are ways I can apply what I have learned in my life?

Review: How would you share this lesson with someone who was not here today?

Summary: I can be content in all situations when I focus on Jesus and the Gospel.

Memory Verse: Philippians 4:8

P.R.A.Y. (<u>P</u>raise, <u>R</u>epent, <u>A</u>sk, and say "<u>Y</u>es" to what God has revealed to you)

Lord's Supper (if you are a church)

Set Goals:
> 1. Share the gospel and what you learned this week
> 2. Read Philippians 4
> 3. Share with group how you will respond to the lesson this week

Gospel of Mark

Passage: Mark 1-3

Vision: "We are a community of baptized believers and seekers of the truth meeting regularly to obey the commands of Scripture and making God's glory known to all peoples." Habakkuk 2:14

Care: How are you doing? Prayer for one another.

Accountability: Review last week's lesson and goals. Did you share with someone?

Worship (song, testimony, tithes/offerings, etc)

New Lesson Context: Mark is one of four true books about the life of Jesus. We call these books "Gospels" because they tell us the Good News about Jesus. This is the shortest Gospel and gives us a quick overview of the life of Jesus.

New Lesson Reading & Questions:
*Passages to study: Mark 1:1-8, 9-11, 14-20; 2:1-7, 8-12
Questions to discover:
1. In context, summarize this passage as a whole?
2. What do we learn about God/Jesus/Holy Spirit?
3. What do we learn about people?
4. Are there any commands to obey or examples to follow?
5. What are ways I can apply what I have learned in my life?

Review: How would you share this lesson with someone who was not here today?

Summary: Jesus came to the earth with the purpose and authority to forgive sins.

Memory Verse: Mark 1:5

P.R.A.Y. (Praise, Repent, Ask, and say "Yes" to what God has revealed to you)

Lord's Supper (if you are a church)

Set Goals:
1. Share the gospel and what you learned this week
2. Read Mark 1-3
3. Share with group how you will respond to the lesson this week

Passage: Mark 4-5

Vision: "We are a community of baptized believers and seekers of the truth meeting regularly to obey the commands of Scripture and making God's glory known to all peoples." Habakkuk 2:14

Care: How are you doing? Prayer for one another.

Accountability: Review last week's lesson and goals. Did you share with someone?

Worship (song, testimony, tithes/offerings, etc)

New Lesson Context: Many times, Jesus taught people using parables. These parables are examples to help us understand a difficult idea. Many of Jesus' parables help us to understand about the Kingdom of God. (Mark 4:33-34)

New Lesson Reading & Questions:
> *Passages to study: Mark 4:1-9,13-20
> Questions to discover:
>> 1. In context, summarize this passage as a whole?
>> 2. What do we learn about God/Jesus/Holy Spirit?
>> 3. What do we learn about people?
>> 4. Are there any commands to obey or examples to follow?
>> 5. What are ways I can apply what I have learned in my life?

Review: How would you share this lesson with someone who was not here today?

Summary: What kind of "soil" am I? The "path", the "rocky ground", the "thorns", or am I "good soil"?

Memory Verse: Mark 4:20

P.R.A.Y. (Praise, Repent, Ask, and say "Yes" to what God has revealed to you)

Lord's Supper (if you are a church)

Set Goals:
> 1. Share the gospel and what you learned this week
> 2. Read Mark 4-5
> 3. Share with group how you will respond to the lesson this week

Passage: Mark 6-7

Vision: "We are a community of baptized believers and seekers of the truth meeting regularly to obey the commands of Scripture and making God's glory known to all peoples." Habakkuk 2:14

Care: How are you doing? Prayer for one another.

Accountability: Review last week's lesson and goals. Did you share with someone?

Worship (song, testimony, tithes/offerings, etc)

New Lesson Context: In chapters 1-6, Jesus performed many miracles. He cast out demons, healed people, fed over 5,000 people with 5 loves of bread and 2 fish, and Jesus even walked on water! Many of the religious leaders, called Pharisees, were jealous of Jesus. They looked religious on the outside, but Jesus could see their hearts (what they were thinking).

New Lesson Reading & Questions:
   *Passages to study: Mark 7:1-5, 6-8, 9-13, 14-16, 17-23
   Questions to discover:
       1. In context, summarize this passage as a whole?
       2. What do we learn about God/Jesus/Holy Spirit?
       3. What do we learn about people?
       4. Are there any commands to obey or examples to follow?
       5. What are ways I can apply what I have learned in my life?

Review: How would you share this lesson with someone who was not here today?

Summary: A true believer is pure in his heart, not just his actions.

Memory Verse: Mark 7:6b-7

P.R.A.Y. (Praise, Repent, Ask, and say "Yes" to what God has revealed to you)

Lord's Supper (if you are a church)

Set Goals:
       1. Share the gospel and what you learned this week
       2. Read Mark 6-7
       3. Share with group how you will respond to the lesson this week

Passage: Mark 8-9

Vision: "We are a community of baptized believers and seekers of the truth meeting regularly to obey the commands of Scripture and making God's glory known to all peoples." Habakkuk 2:14

Care: How are you doing? Prayer for one another.

Accountability: Review last week's lesson and goals. Did you share with someone?

Worship (song, testimony, tithes/offerings, etc)

New Lesson Context: As Jesus taught and did many miracles, people were confused about who Jesus was. Was He a prophet, a king, a teacher, or just a good man?

New Lesson Reading & Questions:
> *Passages to study: Mark 8:27-30, 31-33, 34-38
> Questions to discover:
>> 1. In context, summarize this passage as a whole?
>> 2. What do we learn about God/Jesus/Holy Spirit?
>> 3. What do we learn about people?
>> 4. Are there any commands to obey or examples to follow?
>> 5. What are ways I can apply what I have learned in my life?

Review: How would you share this lesson with someone who was not here today?

Summary: Jesus is the Messiah and I must be willing to give up my life to follow Him.

Memory Verse: Mark 8:35

P.R.A.Y. (Praise, Repent, Ask, and say "Yes" to what God has revealed to you)

Lord's Supper (if you are a church)

Set Goals:
> 1. Share the gospel and what you learned this week
> 2. Read Mark 8-9
> 3. Share with group how you will respond to the lesson this week

Passage: Mark 10-12

Vision: "We are a community of baptized believers and seekers of the truth meeting regularly to obey the commands of Scripture and making God's glory known to all peoples." Habakkuk 2:14

Care: How are you doing? Prayer for one another.

Accountability: Review last week's lesson and goals. Did you share with someone?

Worship (song, testimony, tithes/offerings, etc)

New Lesson Context: As Jesus knew that He would soon die, He began to give final warnings to His followers.

New Lesson Reading & Questions:
> *Passages to study: Mark 10:17-22, 23-31, 32-34, 35-45
> Questions to discover:
>> 1. In context, summarize this passage as a whole?
>> 2. What do we learn about God/Jesus/Holy Spirit?
>> 3. What do we learn about people?
>> 4. Are there any commands to obey or examples to follow?
>> 5. What are ways I can apply what I have learned in my life?

Review: How would you share this lesson with someone who was not here today?

Summary: A follower of Jesus sacrifices everything in this world to gain everything in the Kingdom of God.

Memory Verse: Mark 10:45

P.R.A.Y. (Praise, Repent, Ask, and say "Yes" to what God has revealed to you)

Lord's Supper (if you are a church)

Set Goals:
> 1. Share the gospel and what you learned this week
> 2. Read Mark 10-12
> 3. Share with group how you will respond to the lesson this week

Passage: Mark 13-16

Vision: "We are a community of baptized believers and seekers of the truth meeting regularly to obey the commands of Scripture and making God's glory known to all peoples." Habakkuk 2:14

Care: How are you doing? Prayer for one another.

Accountability: Review last week's lesson and goals. Did you share with someone?

Worship (song, testimony, tithes/offerings, etc)

New Lesson Context: Before Jesus was arrested and killed on a cross, He gave His final teaching about the future.

New Lesson Reading & Questions:
    *Passages to study: Mark 13:1-8, 9-13, 14-23, 24-27, 28-31, 32-37
    Questions to discover:
        1. In context, summarize this passage as a whole?
        2. What do we learn about God/Jesus/Holy Spirit?
        3. What do we learn about people?
        4. Are there any commands to obey or examples to follow?
        5. What are ways I can apply what I have learned in my life?

Review: How would you share this lesson with someone who was not here today?

Summary: We must be faithful and ready because Jesus will return.

Memory Verse: Mark 13:10

P.R.A.Y. (Praise, Repent, Ask, and say "Yes" to what God has revealed to you)

Lord's Supper (if you are a church)

Set Goals:
    1. Share the gospel and what you learned this week
    2. Read Mark 13-16
    3. Share with group how you will respond to the lesson this week

James

Passage: James 1

Vision: "We are a community of baptized believers and seekers of the truth meeting regularly to obey the commands of Scripture and making God's glory known to all peoples." Habakkuk 2:14

Care: How are you doing? Prayer for one another.

Accountability: Review last week's lesson and goals. Did you share with someone?

Worship (song, testimony, tithes/offerings, etc)

New Lesson Context: James wrote this letter to Christians facing persecution. He wrote to encourage them to stay faithful to living out their faith.

New Lesson Reading & Questions:
　　*Passages to study: James 1:2-4, 13-15, 16-18, 19-25, 26-27
　　Questions to discover:
　　　　1. In context, summarize this passage as a whole?
　　　　2. What do we learn about God/Jesus/Holy Spirit?
　　　　3. What do we learn about people?
　　　　4. Are there any commands to obey or examples to follow?
　　　　5. What are ways I can apply what I have learned in my life?

Review: How would you share this lesson with someone who was not here today?

Summary: Even when trials come, I must be faithful to doing what the Bible says.

Memory Verse: James 1:22

P.R.A.Y. (Praise, Repent, Ask, and say "Yes" to what God has revealed to you)

Lord's Supper (if you are a church)

Set Goals:
　　1. Share the gospel and what you learned this week
　　2. Read James 1
　　3. Share with group how you will respond to the lesson this week

Passage: James 2

Vision: "We are a community of baptized believers and seekers of the truth meeting regularly to obey the commands of Scripture and making God's glory known to all peoples." Habakkuk 2:14

Care: How are you doing? Prayer for one another.

Accountability: Review last week's lesson and goals. Did you share with someone?

Worship (song, testimony, tithes/offerings, etc)

New Lesson Context: James wrote this letter to Christians facing persecution. He wrote to encourage them to stay faithful to living out their faith.

New Lesson Reading & Questions:
> *Passages to study: James 2:1-9, 10-13, 14-19, 20-26
> Questions to discover:
>> 1. In context, summarize this passage as a whole?
>> 2. What do we learn about God/Jesus/Holy Spirit?
>> 3. What do we learn about people?
>> 4. Are there any commands to obey or examples to follow?
>> 5. What are ways I can apply what I have learned in my life?

Review: How would you share this lesson with someone who was not here today?

Summary: The evidence of true faith is doing what you say you believe.

Memory Verse: James 2:10

P.R.A.Y. (<u>P</u>raise, <u>R</u>epent, <u>A</u>sk, and say "<u>Y</u>es" to what God has revealed to you)

Lord's Supper (if you are a church)

Set Goals:
> 1. Share the gospel and what you learned this week
> 2. Read James 2
> 3. Share with group how you will respond to the lesson this week

Passage: James 3

Vision: "We are a community of baptized believers and seekers of the truth meeting regularly to obey the commands of Scripture and making God's glory known to all peoples." Habakkuk 2:14

Care: How are you doing? Prayer for one another.

Accountability: Review last week's lesson and goals. Did you share with someone?

Worship (song, testimony, tithes/offerings, etc)

New Lesson Context: James wrote this letter to Christians facing persecution. He wrote to encourage them to stay faithful to living out their faith.

New Lesson Reading & Questions:
> *Passages to study: James 3:1-6, 7-12, 13-18
> Questions to discover:
>> 1. In context, summarize this passage as a whole?
>> 2. What do we learn about God/Jesus/Holy Spirit?
>> 3. What do we learn about people?
>> 4. Are there any commands to obey or examples to follow?
>> 5. What are ways I can apply what I have learned in my life?

Review: How would you share this lesson with someone who was not here today?

Summary: Only the things that are pure should be spoken from a believer's mouth.

Memory Verse: James 3:8

P.R.A.Y. (Praise, Repent, Ask, and say "Yes" to what God has revealed to you)

Lord's Supper (if you are a church)

Set Goals:
> 1. Share the gospel and what you learned this week
> 2. Read James 3
> 3. Share with group how you will respond to the lesson this week

Passage: James 4

Vision: "We are a community of baptized believers and seekers of the truth meeting regularly to obey the commands of Scripture and making God's glory known to all peoples." Habakkuk 2:14

Care: How are you doing? Prayer for one another.

Accountability: Review last week's lesson and goals. Did you share with someone?

Worship (song, testimony, tithes/offerings, etc)

New Lesson Context: James wrote this letter to Christians facing persecution. He wrote to encourage them to stay faithful to living out their faith.

New Lesson Reading & Questions:
  *Passages to study: James 4:1-6, 7-10, 11-12, 13-17
  Questions to discover:
    1. In context, summarize this passage as a whole?
    2. What do we learn about God/Jesus/Holy Spirit?
    3. What do we learn about people?
    4. Are there any commands to obey or examples to follow?
    5. What are ways I can apply what I have learned in my life?

Review: How would you share this lesson with someone who was not here today?

Summary: Every day I should seek to resist the Devil and walk closer to God.

Memory Verse: James 4:17

P.R.A.Y. (Praise, Repent, Ask, and say "Yes" to what God has revealed to you)

Lord's Supper (if you are a church)

Set Goals:
    1. Share the gospel and what you learned this week
    2. Read James 4
    3. Share with group how you will respond to the lesson this week

Passage: James 5

Vision: "We are a community of baptized believers and seekers of the truth meeting regularly to obey the commands of Scripture and making God's glory known to all peoples." Habakkuk 2:14

Care: How are you doing? Prayer for one another.

Accountability: Review last week's lesson and goals. Did you share with someone?

Worship (song, testimony, tithes/offerings, etc)

New Lesson Context: James wrote this letter to Christians facing persecution. He wrote to encourage them to stay faithful to living out their faith.

New Lesson Reading & Questions:
   *Passages to study: James 5:1-6, 7-11, 13-20
   Questions to discover:
      1. In context, summarize this passage as a whole?
      2. What do we learn about God/Jesus/Holy Spirit?
      3. What do we learn about people?
      4. Are there any commands to obey or examples to follow?
      5. What are ways I can apply what I have learned in my life?

Review: How would you share this lesson with someone who was not here today?

Summary: A Christian isn't only concerned with himself, but prays with believers and keeps other believers accountable as well.

Memory Verse: James 5:16

P.R.A.Y. (Praise, Repent, Ask, and say "Yes" to what God has revealed to you)

Lord's Supper (if you are a church)

Set Goals:
      1. Share the gospel and what you learned this week
      2. Read James 5
      3. Share with group how you will respond to the lesson this week

Gospel of Matthew

Passage: Matthew 5

**Matthew 5:1-16 are not covered in this study. This can be added in as the first lesson in the book of Matthew as an option.

Vision: "We are a community of baptized believers and seekers of the truth meeting regularly to obey the commands of Scripture and making God's glory known to all peoples." Habakkuk 2:14

Care: How are you doing? Prayer for one another.

Accountability: Review last week's lesson and goals. Did you share with someone?

Worship (song, testimony, tithes/offerings, etc)

New Lesson Context: In this series, we are looking at some of Jesus' teachings in the book of Matthew. During this time, many Jewish people thought they were righteous because they obeyed many of God's laws. But, (unlike the religious leaders) God didn't want them to only obey with their actions, but with their hearts. (Matt 5:17-20)

New Lesson Reading & Questions:
  *Passages to study: Matthew 5:21-26, 27-32, 33-37, 38-48
  Questions to discover:
      1. In context, summarize this passage as a whole?
      2. What do we learn about God/Jesus/Holy Spirit?
      3. What do we learn about people?
      4. Are there any commands to obey or examples to follow?
      5. What are ways I can apply what I have learned in my life?

Review: How would you share this lesson with someone who was not here today?

Summary: I must follow God, not just with my outward actions, but with the way I act and think.

Memory Verse: Matthew 5:16

P.R.A.Y. (Praise, Repent, Ask, and say "Yes" to what God has revealed to you)

Lord's Supper (if you are a church)

Set Goals:
      1. Share the gospel and what you learned this week
      2. Read Matthew 1-4
      3. Share with group how you will respond to the lesson this week

Passage: Matthew 6:1-18

Vision: "We are a community of baptized believers and seekers of the truth meeting regularly to obey the commands of Scripture and making God's glory known to all peoples." Habakkuk 2:14

Care: How are you doing? Prayer for one another.

Accountability: Review last week's lesson and goals. Did you share with someone?

Worship (song, testimony, tithes/offerings, etc)

New Lesson Context: In this series, we are looking at some of Jesus' teachings in the book of Matthew. During this time, the religious leaders did many good deeds so other people could see them and praise them. Again, Jesus taught that the attitude of your heart is more important than your actions.

New Lesson Reading & Questions:
> *Passages to study: Matthew 6:1-4, 5-15, 16-18
> Questions to discover:
>> 1. In context, summarize this passage as a whole?
>> 2. What do we learn about God/Jesus/Holy Spirit?
>> 3. What do we learn about people?
>> 4. Are there any commands to obey or examples to follow?
>> 5. What are ways I can apply what I have learned in my life?

Review: How would you share this lesson with someone who was not here today?

Summary: I must follow God, not just with my outward actions, but with the way I act and think. (same as last week...a more specific summary can be given if needed)

Memory Verse: Matthew 6:1

P.R.A.Y. (Praise, Repent, Ask, and say "Yes" to what God has revealed to you)

Lord's Supper (if you are a church)

Set Goals:
1. Share the gospel and what you learned this week
2. Read Matthew 8-11
3. Share with group how you will respond to the lesson this week

Passage: Matthew 6:19-34

Vision: "We are a community of baptized believers and seekers of the truth meeting regularly to obey the commands of Scripture and making God's glory known to all peoples." Habakkuk 2:14

Care: How are you doing? Prayer for one another.

Accountability: Review last week's lesson and goals. Did you share with someone?

Worship (song, testimony, tithes/offerings, etc)

New Lesson Context: In this series, we are looking at some of Jesus' teachings in the book of Matthew. After Jesus showed the religious people that they had sin in their hearts (even when their actions were good), Jesus explained that we must change our desires.

New Lesson Reading & Questions:
> *Passages to study: Matthew 6:19-24, 25-34
> Questions to discover:
>> 1. In context, summarize this passage as a whole?
>> 2. What do we learn about God/Jesus/Holy Spirit?
>> 3. What do we learn about people?
>> 4. Are there any commands to obey or examples to follow?
>> 5. What are ways I can apply what I have learned in my life?

Review: How would you share this lesson with someone who was not here today?

Summary: Our desire should be on the Kingdom of God, not the things of this world.

Memory Verse: Matthew 6:33

P.R.A.Y. (Praise, Repent, Ask, and say "Yes" to what God has revealed to you)

Lord's Supper (if you are a church)

Set Goals:
> 1. Share the gospel and what you learned this week
> 2. Read Matthew 12-14
> 3. Share with group how you will respond to the lesson this week

Passage: Matthew 7

Vision: "We are a community of baptized believers and seekers of the truth meeting regularly to obey the commands of Scripture and making God's glory known to all peoples." Habakkuk 2:14

Care: How are you doing? Prayer for one another.

Accountability: Review last week's lesson and goals. Did you share with someone?

Worship (song, testimony, tithes/offerings, etc)

New Lesson Context: In this series, we are looking at some of Jesus' teachings in the book of Matthew. Many people believed there were many ways to enter the Kingdom of God and find salvation. Jesus taught the people about the only path leads to God.

New Lesson Reading & Questions:
>*Passages to study: Matthew 7:13-23, 24-29
>Questions to discover:
>>1. In context, summarize this passage as a whole?
>>2. What do we learn about God/Jesus/Holy Spirit?
>>3. What do we learn about people?
>>4. Are there any commands to obey or examples to follow?
>>5. What are ways I can apply what I have learned in my life?

Review: How would you share this lesson with someone who was not here today?

Summary: There is only 1 path to God. This path is through the narrow gate and it is built on a solid foundation.

Memory Verse: Matthew 7:14

P.R.A.Y. (Praise, Repent, Ask, and say "Yes" to what God has revealed to you)

Lord's Supper (if you are a church)

Set Goals:
>1. Share the gospel and what you learned this week
>2. Read Matthew 15-18
>3. Share with group how you will respond to the lesson this week

Passage: Matthew 24

Vision: "We are a community of baptized believers and seekers of the truth meeting regularly to obey the commands of Scripture and making God's glory known to all peoples." Habakkuk 2:14

Care: How are you doing? Prayer for one another.

Accountability: Review last week's lesson and goals. Did you share with someone?

Worship (song, testimony, tithes/offerings, etc)

New Lesson Context: The last teaching Jesus gave His disciples was about the future. Jesus prophesied about His death and resurrection. He also prophesied about His return and the end of the world. Finally, Jesus gave many warnings about the future for both His disciples and also for all believers.

New Lesson Reading & Questions:
>*Passages to study: Matthew 24:1-14, 23-28, 36-44, 45-51
>Questions to discover:
>>1. In context, summarize this passage as a whole?
>>2. What do we learn about God/Jesus/Holy Spirit?
>>3. What do we learn about people?
>>4. Are there any commands to obey or examples to follow?
>>5. What are ways I can apply what I have learned in my life?

Review: How would you share this lesson with someone who was not here today?

Summary: No one knows when Jesus will return, but we must be ready and prepared to share the gospel to all peoples as we wait for His return.

Memory Verse: Matthew 24:14

P.R.A.Y. (Praise, Repent, Ask, and say "Yes" to what God has revealed to you)

Lord's Supper (if you are a church)

Set Goals:
>1. Share the gospel and what you learned this week
>2. Read Matthew 19-22
>3. Share with group how you will respond to the lesson this week

Passage: Matthew 25

Vision: "We are a community of baptized believers and seekers of the truth meeting regularly to obey the commands of Scripture and making God's glory known to all peoples." Habakkuk 2:14

Care: How are you doing? Prayer for one another.

Accountability: Review last week's lesson and goals. Did you share with someone?

Worship (song, testimony, tithes/offerings, etc)

New Lesson Context: The last teaching Jesus gave His disciples was about the future. Jesus continued His teaching, reminding the believers to be ready for the end. Also, Jesus warned that at the end of time, believers and unbelievers will be eternally separated.

New Lesson Reading & Questions:
>   *Passages to study: Matthew 25:1-13, 31-46
>   Questions to discover:
>> 1. In context, summarize this passage as a whole?
>> 2. What do we learn about God/Jesus/Holy Spirit?
>> 3. What do we learn about people?
>> 4. Are there any commands to obey or examples to follow?
>> 5. What are ways I can apply what I have learned in my life?

Review: How would you share this lesson with someone who was not here today?

Summary: After this life, we will receive eternal punishment or eternal life with God. We must not wait to make our choice.

Memory Verse: Matthew 25:13

P.R.A.Y. (Praise, Repent, Ask, and say "Yes" to what God has revealed to you)

Lord's Supper (if you are a church)

Set Goals:
>   1. Share the gospel and what you learned this week
>   2. Read Matthew 23-25
>   3. Share with group how you will respond to the lesson this week

Passage: Matthew 26-28

Vision: "We are a community of baptized believers and seekers of the truth meeting regularly to obey the commands of Scripture and making God's glory known to all peoples." Habakkuk 2:14

Care: How are you doing? Prayer for one another.

Accountability: Review last week's lesson and goals. Did you share with someone?

Worship (song, testimony, tithes/offerings, etc)

New Lesson Context: The religious leaders thought they could get rid of Jesus and prove that He was not the Messiah by killing Jesus on a cross.

New Lesson Reading & Questions:
>   *Passages to study: Matthew 27:57-66; 28:1-10, 11-15, 16-20
>   Questions to discover:
>   1. In context, summarize this passage as a whole?
>   2. What do we learn about God/Jesus/Holy Spirit?
>   3. What do we learn about people?
>   4. Are there any commands to obey or examples to follow?
>   5. What are ways I can apply what I have learned in my life?

Review: How would you share this lesson with someone who was not here today?

Summary: Because Jesus is alive, we are commanded and enabled to spread this Good News and make disciples of all peoples.

Memory Verse: Matthew 28:18-20

P.R.A.Y. (Praise, Repent, Ask, and say "Yes" to what God has revealed to you)

Lord's Supper (if you are a church)

Set Goals:
>   1. Share the gospel and what you learned this week
>   2. Read Matthew 26-28
>   3. Share with group how you will respond to the lesson this week

Ephesians

Passage: Ephesians 1-2

Vision: "We are a community of baptized believers and seekers of the truth meeting regularly to obey the commands of Scripture and making God's glory known to all peoples." Habakkuk 2:14

Care: How are you doing? Prayer for one another.

Accountability: Review last week's lesson and goals. Did you share with someone?

Worship (song, testimony, tithes/offerings, etc)

New Lesson Context: Paul wrote a letter to a church in the city of Ephesus. In chapter 1, he reminded them of who they are in Christ. In chapter 2, Paul reminded them of who they were before knowing Christ and how they came to Christ. Finally, Paul concluded chapter 2, explaining how these things should unite them as a church.

New Lesson Reading & Questions:
>*Passages to study: Ephesians 1:20-23; 2:1-10
>Questions to discover:
>>1. In context, summarize this passage as a whole?
>>2. What do we learn about God/Jesus/Holy Spirit?
>>3. What do we learn about people?
>>4. Are there any commands to obey or examples to follow?
>>5. What are ways I can apply what I have learned in my life?

Review: How would you share this lesson with someone who was not here today?

Summary: We were dead in our sins, but by God's grace, He made us alive with Christ.

Memory Verse: Ephesians 2:8-9

P.R.A.Y. (Praise, Repent, Ask, and say "Yes" to what God has revealed to you)

Lord's Supper (if you are a church)

Set Goals:
>1. Share the gospel and what you learned this week
>2. Read Ephesians 1-2
>3. Share with group how you will respond to the lesson this week

Passage: Ephesians 3

Vision: "We are a community of baptized believers and seekers of the truth meeting regularly to obey the commands of Scripture and making God's glory known to all peoples." Habakkuk 2:14

Care: How are you doing? Prayer for one another.

Accountability: Review last week's lesson and goals. Did you share with someone?

Worship (song, testimony, tithes/offerings, etc)

New Lesson Context: Paul had reminded the church of their new life in Christ and how this should unite the their church together. In chapter 3, Paul explained how the gospel is for both Jews and Gentiles (all people) and how this is for God's glory and part of God's plan. Read Ephesians 3:8-13. Finally, Paul prayed for the believers.

New Lesson Reading & Questions:
>*Passages to study: Ephesians 3:1-13, 14-19, 20-21
>Questions to discover:
>>1. In context, summarize this passage as a whole?
>>2. What do we learn about God/Jesus/Holy Spirit?
>>3. What do we learn about people?
>>4. Are there any commands to obey or examples to follow?
>>5. What are ways I can apply what I have learned in my life?

Review: How would you share this lesson with someone who was not here today?

Summary: God desires for me to be "grounded" in my faith and love for Christ and for others. This comes through the power of the Holy Spirit.

Memory Verse: Ephesians 3:20

P.R.A.Y. (Praise, Repent, Ask, and say "Yes" to what God has revealed to you)

Lord's Supper (if you are a church)

Set Goals:
>1. Share the gospel and what you learned this week
>2. Read Ephesians 3
>3. Share with group how you will respond to the lesson this week

Passage: Ephesians 4:1-5:5

Vision: "We are a community of baptized believers and seekers of the truth meeting regularly to obey the commands of Scripture and making God's glory known to all peoples." Habakkuk 2:14

Care: How are you doing? Prayer for one another.

Accountability: Review last week's lesson and goals. Did you share with someone?

Worship (song, testimony, tithes/offerings, etc)

New Lesson Context: Because of all that Jesus has done for us, Paul challenged believers to "walk worthy" of Jesus. He then gave some examples of how a Christian should "walk worthy" of Jesus.

New Lesson Reading & Questions:
    *Passages to study: Ephesians 4:1-6, 15-16, 4:25-5:2; 5:3-5
    Questions to discover:
        1. In context, summarize this passage as a whole?
        2. What do we learn about God/Jesus/Holy Spirit?
        3. What do we learn about people?
        4. Are there any commands to obey or examples to follow?
        5. What are ways I can apply what I have learned in my life?

Review: How would you share this lesson with someone who was not here today?

Summary: Believers are to honor Jesus by the way they live their lives. Also, we are to grow in our "new life" with other believers in the context of a local church.

Memory Verse: Ephesians 4:1-3

P.R.A.Y. (<u>P</u>raise, <u>R</u>epent, <u>A</u>sk, and say "<u>Y</u>es" to what God has revealed to you)

Lord's Supper (if you are a church)

Set Goals:
    1. Share the gospel and what you learned this week
    2. Read Ephesians 4
    3. Share with group how you will respond to the lesson this week

Passage: Ephesians 5:6-6:9

Vision: "We are a community of baptized believers and seekers of the truth meeting regularly to obey the commands of Scripture and making God's glory known to all peoples." Habakkuk 2:14

Care: How are you doing? Prayer for one another.

Accountability: Review last week's lesson and goals. Did you share with someone?

Worship (song, testimony, tithes/offerings, etc)

New Lesson Context: Paul continued to remind the believers that they should now "walk in the light". They should live their lives in a way that brings honor to Jesus and spreads His light to all people. One area that we can be a light to people around us is in our relationships with our family and those in our jobs.

New Lesson Reading & Questions:
> *Passages to study: Ephesians 5:22-33; 6:1-4, 5-9
> Questions to discover:
>> 1. In context, summarize this passage as a whole?
>> 2. What do we learn about God/Jesus/Holy Spirit?
>> 3. What do we learn about people?
>> 4. Are there any commands to obey or examples to follow?
>> 5. What are ways I can apply what I have learned in my life?

Review: How would you share this lesson with someone who was not here today?

Summary: We can show the world God's light by honoring God in our family and at our work.

Memory Verse: Ephesians 5:15-16

P.R.A.Y. (Praise, Repent, Ask, and say "Yes" to what God has revealed to you)

Lord's Supper (if you are a church)

Set Goals:
> 1. Share the gospel and what you learned this week
> 2. Read Ephesians 5
> 3. Share with group how you will respond to the lesson this week

Passage: Ephesians 6:10-24

Vision: "We are a community of baptized believers and seekers of the truth meeting regularly to obey the commands of Scripture and making God's glory known to all peoples." Habakkuk 2:14

Care: How are you doing? Prayer for one another.

Accountability: Review last week's lesson and goals. Did you share with someone?

Worship (song, testimony, tithes/offerings, etc)

New Lesson Context: Finally, Paul gave a final reminder about how to "walk in the light". It is not something we can do on our own, so we must trust in God to help us do it. Paul gave an example of the armor of a soldier to help us understand how we can stand against the Devil and walk in the light.

New Lesson Reading & Questions:
>*Passages to study: Ephesians 6:1-13, 14-18, 19-20
>Questions to discover:
>>1. In context, summarize this passage as a whole?
>>2. What do we learn about God/Jesus/Holy Spirit?
>>3. What do we learn about people?
>>4. Are there any commands to obey or examples to follow?
>>5. What are ways I can apply what I have learned in my life?

Review: How would you share this lesson with someone who was not here today?

Summary: I must trust in God by putting on "spiritual" armor as I face the temptations and sins of the Devil and the world.

Memory Verse: Ephesians 6:11

P.R.A.Y. (Praise, Repent, Ask, and say "Yes" to what God has revealed to you)

Lord's Supper (if you are a church)

Set Goals:
>1. Share the gospel and what you learned this week
>2. Read Ephesians 6
>3. Share with group how you will respond to the lesson this week

Romans

Passage: Romans 1

Vision: "We are a community of baptized believers and seekers of the truth meeting regularly to obey the commands of Scripture and making God's glory known to all peoples." Habakkuk 2:14

Care: How are you doing? Prayer for one another.

Accountability: Review last week's lesson and goals. Did you share with someone?

Worship (song, testimony, tithes/offerings, etc)

New Lesson Context: (Romans 1:1-17) Before traveling to Rome, Paul wrote the church in Rome a letter to clarify the gospel. Among the believers in Rome, there was confusion over Jews and Gentiles being equal in Christianity. Paul wrote the church in Rome to explain that the gospel is for all people (Romans 1:16).

New Lesson Reading & Questions:
    *Passages to study: Romans 1:16-17, 18-20; 21-25; 26-32
    Questions to discover:
        1. In context, summarize this passage as a whole?
        2. What do we learn about God/Jesus/Holy Spirit?
        3. What do we learn about people?
        4. Are there any commands to obey or examples to follow?
        5. What are ways I can apply what I have learned in my life?

Review: How would you share this lesson with someone who was not here today?

Summary: We were created to worship the Creator, not the creation.

Memory Verse: Romans 1:20

P.R.A.Y. (Praise, Repent, Ask, and say "Yes" to what God has revealed to you)

Lord's Supper (if you are a church)

Set Goals:
    1. Share the gospel and what you learned this week
    2. Read Romans 1
    3. Share with group how you will respond to the lesson this week

Passage: Romans 2-3

Vision: "We are a community of baptized believers and seekers of the truth meeting regularly to obey the commands of Scripture and making God's glory known to all peoples." Habakkuk 2:14

Care: How are you doing? Prayer for one another.

Accountability: Review last week's lesson and goals. Did you share with someone?

Worship (song, testimony, tithes/offerings, etc)

New Lesson Context: The former Jews in the church thought they were better than the Gentiles (Romans 2:1). The former Jews thought they were more "righteous" because they followed many religious laws.

New Lesson Reading & Questions:
    *Passages to study: Romans 3:9-12, 13-19, 20-22, 23-27
    Questions to discover:
            1. In context, summarize this passage as a whole?
            2. What do we learn about God/Jesus/Holy Spirit?
            3. What do we learn about people?
            4. Are there any commands to obey or examples to follow?
            5. What are ways I can apply what I have learned in my life?

Review: How would you share this lesson with someone who was not here today?

Summary: No matter how many good things we have done, no one is righteous before God. All people have sin.

Memory Verse: Romans 3:23

P.R.A.Y. (Praise, Repent, Ask, and say "Yes" to what God has revealed to you)

Lord's Supper (if you are a church)

Set Goals:
    1. Share the gospel and what you learned this week
    2. Read Romans 2-3
    3. Share with group how you will respond to the lesson this week

Passage: Romans 4-5

Vision: "We are a community of baptized believers and seekers of the truth meeting regularly to obey the commands of Scripture and making God's glory known to all peoples." Habakkuk 2:14

Care: How are you doing? Prayer for one another.

Accountability: Review last week's lesson and goals. Did you share with someone?

Worship (song, testimony, tithes/offerings, etc)

New Lesson Context: Abraham is considered the "Father" of the Jewish faith. So, Paul showed how it wasn't Abraham's works or good deeds that made him righteous.

New Lesson Reading & Questions:
> *Passages to study: Romans 4:1-5; 5:1-5, 6-11
> Questions to discover:
>> 1. In context, summarize this passage as a whole?
>> 2. What do we learn about God/Jesus/Holy Spirit?
>> 3. What do we learn about people?
>> 4. Are there any commands to obey or examples to follow?
>> 5. What are ways I can apply what I have learned in my life?

Review: How would you share this lesson with someone who was not here today?

Summary: Only through faith in Jesus can we be made righteous before God.

Memory Verse: Romans 5:1

P.R.A.Y. (Praise, Repent, Ask, and say "Yes" to what God has revealed to you)

Lord's Supper (if you are a church)

Set Goals:
> 1. Share the gospel and what you learned this week
> 2. Read Romans 4-5
> 3. Share with group how you will respond to the lesson this week

Passage: Romans 6-7

Vision: "We are a community of baptized believers and seekers of the truth meeting regularly to obey the commands of Scripture and making God's glory known to all peoples." Habakkuk 2:14

Care: How are you doing? Prayer for one another.

Accountability: Review last week's lesson and goals. Did you share with someone?

Worship (song, testimony, tithes/offerings, etc)

New Lesson Context: After explaining that all people are sinners, but become righteous though faith in Christ, Paul answered the question, "If righteousness comes by faith, then does this mean that we can sin and live however we want since God will forgive us?"

New Lesson Reading & Questions:
>*Passages to study: Romans 6:1-14; 7:18-25
>Questions to discover:
>>1. In context, summarize this passage as a whole?
>>2. What do we learn about God/Jesus/Holy Spirit?
>>3. What do we learn about people?
>>4. Are there any commands to obey or examples to follow?
>>5. What are ways I can apply what I have learned in my life?

Review: How would you share this lesson with someone who was not here today?

Summary: I am a sinner who has been given a new life in Christ, no longer living in sin.

Memory Verse: Romans 6:23

P.R.A.Y. (Praise, Repent, Ask, and say "Yes" to what God has revealed to you)

Lord's Supper (if you are a church)

Set Goals:
>1. Share the gospel and what you learned this week
>2. Read Romans 6-7
>3. Share with group how you will respond to the lesson this week

Passage: Romans 8-11

Vision: "We are a community of baptized believers and seekers of the truth meeting regularly to obey the commands of Scripture and making God's glory known to all peoples." Habakkuk 2:14

Care: How are you doing? Prayer for one another.

Accountability: Review last week's lesson and goals. Did you share with someone?

Worship (song, testimony, tithes/offerings, etc)

New Lesson Context: The book of Romans reminds us that we are all sinners and are not righteous through the things we do or in our own power. Paul reminded us of this in Romans 7:24. Then, Paul explained how we can live a life that pleases God.

New Lesson Reading & Questions:
>   *Passages to study: Romans 8:1-2, 3-8, 9-11, 12-17, 26-27
>   Questions to discover:
>>   1. In context, summarize this passage as a whole?
>>   2. What do we learn about God/Jesus/Holy Spirit?
>>   3. What do we learn about people?
>>   4. Are there any commands to obey or examples to follow?
>>   5. What are ways I can apply what I have learned in my life?

Review: How would you share this lesson with someone who was not here today?

Summary: The children of God have the Spirit of God so we can live a life that pleases God.

Memory Verse: Romans 8:1

P.R.A.Y. (Praise, Repent, Ask, and say "Yes" to what God has revealed to you)

Lord's Supper (if you are a church)

Set Goals:
>   1. Share the gospel and what you learned this week
>   2. Read Romans 8-11
>   3. Share with group how you will respond to the lesson this week

Passage: Romans 12-16

Vision: "We are a community of baptized believers and seekers of the truth meeting regularly to obey the commands of Scripture and making God's glory known to all peoples." Habakkuk 2:14

Care: How are you doing? Prayer for one another.

Accountability: Review last week's lesson and goals. Did you share with someone?

Worship (song, testimony, tithes/offerings, etc)

New Lesson Context: In chapters 1-11, Paul explained our sinfulness and how we can only be righteous through faith in Christ. We then are able to live in obedience to Christ through the Spirit. He then finished the book showing how the truths of the gospel personally led Paul to proclaim this Good News to the ends of the earth. We cannot live the Christian life without first understanding our sinfulness and need for Christ.

New Lesson Reading & Questions:
*Passages to study: Romans 12:1-2, 3-8, 9-15, 16-21
Questions to discover:
1. In context, summarize this passage as a whole?
2. What do we learn about God/Jesus/Holy Spirit?
3. What do we learn about people?
4. Are there any commands to obey or examples to follow?
5. What are ways I can apply what I have learned in my life?

Review: How would you share this lesson with someone who was not here today?

Summary: As a believer, I must not live like the world, but be an example of Christ to the world.

Memory Verse: Romans 12:1-2

P.R.A.Y. (Praise, Repent, Ask, and say "Yes" to what God has revealed to you)

Lord's Supper (if you are a church)

Set Goals:
1. Share the gospel and what you learned this week
2. Read Romans 12-16
3. Share with group how you will respond to the lesson this week

Foundations

Topic: SALVATION

Vision: "We are a community of baptized believers and seekers of the truth meeting regularly to obey the commands of Scripture and making God's glory known to all peoples." Habakkuk 2:14

Care: How are you doing? Prayer for one another.

Accountability: Review last week's lesson and goals. Did you share with someone?

Worship (song, testimony, tithes/offerings, etc)

New Lesson Reading & Questions:
> *Study the following passages on salvation: John 1:11-13; John 3:1-21; John 11:25-26; Romans 3:23; Romans 6:6-10; 23; Romans 10:9-13; 2 Corinthians 5:17; Ephesians 2:1-10; 1 John 1:5-2:2
> Questions to discover:
>> 1. In context, summarize this passage as a whole?
>> 2. What do we learn about God/Jesus/Holy Spirit?
>> 3. What do we learn about people?
>> 4. Are there any commands to obey or examples to follow?
>> 5. What are ways I can apply what I have learned in my life?

Review: How would you share this lesson with someone who was not here today?

Summary: Through salvation, you can have a relationship with a perfect and holy God as your sins have been forgiven. Salvation is offered to all people, but it is something that each person must choose to accept. There is nothing any person can do to earn salvation. Therefore, God became a man (Jesus) and came to us, lived a perfect life, died as a payment for our sins, and rose again from the dead. The Bible teaches that we must accept and believe in this Good News, repent from our sins, and choose to follow Christ for salvation.

Memory Verse:

P.R.A.Y. (Praise, Repent, Ask, and say "Yes" to what God has revealed to you)

Lord's Supper (if you are a church)

Set Goals:
> 1. Share the gospel and what you learned this week
> 2. Read over these passages again at home
> 3. Share with group how you will respond to the lesson this week

Topic: FOLLOWING JESUS

Vision: "We are a community of baptized believers and seekers of the truth meeting regularly to obey the commands of Scripture and making God's glory known to all peoples." Habakkuk 2:14

Care: How are you doing? Prayer for one another.

Accountability: Review last week's lesson and goals. Did you share with someone?

Worship (song, testimony, tithes/offerings, etc)

New Lesson Reading & Questions:
> *Study the following passages on following Jesus: Matthew 7:13-14; Mark 8:34-38; John 14:6; Acts 4:12; 2 Corinthians 5:15; 1 Timothy 2:5-6
> Questions to discover:
>> 1. In context, summarize this passage as a whole?
>> 2. What do we learn about God/Jesus/Holy Spirit?
>> 3. What do we learn about people?
>> 4. Are there any commands to obey or examples to follow?
>> 5. What are ways I can apply what I have learned in my life?

Review: How would you share this lesson with someone who was not here today?

Summary: Because God is perfect, He decides how we can have a relationship with Him for salvation. He gave us clear instructions on how to do this in His Word (the Bible). The Bible says there are many paths, but only one leads to God, and that is through Jesus. Jesus said about Himself, "I am the Way, the Truth, and the Life. Now one can come to the Father (God) but by/through me." Jesus also taught that becoming a follower of Jesus will not be easy. Often, your friends and family will be against you. Difficult times and persecutions will come. In these times, God promises us that He will be with us and guide us with His Spirit.

Memory Verse:

P.R.A.Y. (Praise, Repent, Ask, and say "Yes" to what God has revealed to you)

Lord's Supper (if you are a church)

Set Goals:
1. Share the gospel and what you learned this week
2. Read over these passages again at home
3. Share with group how you will respond to the lesson this week

Topic: BAPTISM

Vision: "We are a community of baptized believers and seekers of the truth meeting regularly to obey the commands of Scripture and making God's glory known to all peoples." Habakkuk 2:14

Care: How are you doing? Prayer for one another.

Accountability: Review last week's lesson and goals. Did you share with someone?

Worship (song, testimony, tithes/offerings, etc)

New Lesson Reading & Questions:
> *Study the following passages on Baptism: Matthew 28:16-20; Acts 2:37-42; Acts 8:35-39; Acts 16:25-34; Romans 6:1-9
> Questions to discover:
>> 1. In context, summarize this passage as a whole?
>> 2. What do we learn about God/Jesus/Holy Spirit?
>> 3. What do we learn about people?
>> 4. Are there any commands to obey or examples to follow?
>> 5. What are ways I can apply what I have learned in my life?

Review: How would you share this lesson with someone who was not here today?

Summary: Baptism is immersion in water after becoming a follower of Jesus. It is an act of obedience that is a symbol of the believer's faith in Jesus being crucified, buried, and risen, the believer's death to sin, and the burial of the old life. It also symbolizes that believers will be resurrected after this life to spend eternity with God.

Memory Verse:

P.R.A.Y. (Praise, Repent, Ask, and say "Yes" to what God has revealed to you)

Lord's Supper (if you are a church)

Set Goals:
> 1. Share the gospel and what you learned this week
> 2. Read over these passages again at home
> 3. Share with group how you will respond to the lesson this week

Topic: TELLING OTHERS

Vision: "We are a community of baptized believers and seekers of the truth meeting regularly to obey the commands of Scripture and making God's glory known to all peoples." Habakkuk 2:14

Care: How are you doing? Prayer for one another.

Accountability: Review last week's lesson and goals. Did you share with someone?

Worship (song, testimony, tithes/offerings, etc)

New Lesson Reading & Questions:
>   *Study the following passages on telling others about Jesus: Matthew 5:13-16; Matthew 28:16-20; Mark 5:18-20; John 4:25-30; 39-42; Romans 1:16; Romans 10:8-15; 2 Corinthians 4:1-6; 2 Timothy 2:2; 1 Peter 3:13-17
>   Questions to discover:
>   1. In context, summarize this passage as a whole?
>   2. What do we learn about God/Jesus/Holy Spirit?
>   3. What do we learn about people?
>   4. Are there any commands to obey or examples to follow?
>   5. What are ways I can apply what I have learned in my life?

Review: How would you share this lesson with someone who was not here today?

Summary: God's children are not ashamed of Him and boldly share with others the Good News of how Jesus has changed their life. This Good News is for all people, races, nationalities, and languages. God gives us His Spirit to give us the words to say and strength to speak His truth to the world.

Memory Verse:

P.R.A.Y. (Praise, Repent, Ask, and say "Yes" to what God has revealed to you)

Lord's Supper (if you are a church)

Set Goals:
1. Share the gospel and what you learned this week
2. Read over these passages again at home
3. Share with group how you will respond to the lesson this week

Topic: CHURCH

Vision: "We are a community of baptized believers and seekers of the truth meeting regularly to obey the commands of Scripture and making God's glory known to all peoples." Habakkuk 2:14

Care: How are you doing? Prayer for one another.

Accountability: Review last week's lesson and goals. Did you share with someone?

Worship (song, testimony, tithes/offerings, etc)

New Lesson Reading & Questions:
   *Study the following passages on church: Matthew 26:26-30; Acts 2:37-47;
   1 Corinthians 11:17-32; 1 Timothy 3:1-13; Titus 1:5-9; 2:1-8
   Questions to discover:
       1. In context, summarize this passage as a whole?
       2. What do we learn about God/Jesus/Holy Spirit?
       3. What do we learn about people?
       4. Are there any commands to obey or examples to follow?
       5. What are ways I can apply what I have learned in my life?

Review: How would you share this lesson with someone who was not here today?

Summary: God wants His children to grow in their relationship with Him through a local church. This is a group of baptized believers who study God's Word, serve, worship together, and make God's glory known to all people. The Bible teaches that there is a pastor who leads the church. The church serves to build up the believers and to share the Good News with unbelievers. The church is also commanded to remember Jesus' death, burial, and resurrection through the taking of "The Lord's Supper".

Memory Verse:

P.R.A.Y. (Praise, Repent, Ask, and say "Yes" to what God has revealed to you)

Lord's Supper (if you are a church)

Set Goals:
       1. Share the gospel and what you learned this week
       2. Read over these passages again at home
       3. Share with group how you will respond to the lesson this week

Biblical Doctrine

DOCTRINE 1
We Believe in the Bible

The Holy Bible was written by men divinely inspired and is God's revelation of Himself to mankind. It is a perfect treasure of divine instruction. It has God for its author, salvation for its end, and truth, without any mixture of error, for its matter. Therefore, all Scripture is totally true and trustworthy. It reveals the principles by which God judges us, and therefore is, and will remain to the end of the world, the true center of Christian union, and the supreme standard by which all human conduct, creeds, and religious opinions should be tried. All Scripture is a testimony to Christ, who is Himself the focus of divine revelation. The Bible is the complete and final prophetic Word of God and is not to be added to or taken away from.

(Exodus 24:4; Deuteronomy 4:1-2; 17:19; Joshua 8:34; Psalms 19:7-10; 119:11,89,105,140; Isaiah 34:16; 40:8; Jeremiah 15:16; 36:1-32; Matthew 5:17-18; 22:29; Luke 21:33; 24:44-46; John 5:39; 16:13-15; 17:17; Acts 2:16ff.; 17:11; Romans 15:4; 16:25-26; 2 Timothy 3:15-17; Hebrews 1:1-2; 4:12; 1 Peter 1:25; 2 Peter 1:19-21; Revelation 22:18-19)

DOCTRINE 2
We Believe in God

There is one and only one living and true God. He is an intelligent, spiritual, and personal Being; the Creator, Redeemer, Preserver, and Ruler of the universe. God is infinite in holiness and all other perfections. God is all powerful and all knowing; and His perfect knowledge extends to all things, past, present, and future, including the future decisions of His free creatures. To Him we owe the highest love, reverence, and obedience. The eternal triune God reveals Himself to us as Father, Son, and Holy Spirit, with distinct personal attributes, but without division of nature, essence, or being.

God the Father. God as Father reigns with providential care over His universe, His creatures, and the flow of the stream of human history according to the purposes of His grace. He is all powerful, all knowing, all loving, and all wise. God is Father in truth to those who become children of God through faith in Jesus Christ. He is fatherly in His attitude toward all mankind.

(Genesis 1:1; 2:7; Exodus 3:14; 6:2-3; 15:11; 20:1; Leviticus 22:2; Deuteronomy 6:4; 32:6; 1 Chronicles 29:10; Psalm 19:1-3; Isaiah 43:3,15; 64:8; Jeremiah 10:10; 17:13; Matthew 6:9; 7:11; 23:9; 28:19; Mark 1:9-11; John 4:24; 5:26; 14:6-13; 17:1-8; Acts 1:7; Romans 8:14-15; 1 Corinthians 8:6; Galatians 4:6; Ephesians 4:6; Colossians 1:15; 1 Timothy 1:17; Hebrews 11:6; 12:9; 1 Peter 1:17; 1 John 5:7)

God the Son. Christ is the eternal Son of God. In His incarnation as Jesus Christ He was conceived of the Holy Spirit and born of the virgin Mary. Jesus perfectly revealed and did the will of God, taking upon Himself human nature with its demands and necessities and identifying Himself completely with mankind yet without sin. He honored the divine law by His personal obedience, and in His substitutionary death on the cross He made provision for the redemption of mankind from sin. He was raised from the dead with a glorified body and appeared to His disciples as the person who was with them before His crucifixion. He ascended into heaven and is now exalted at the right hand of God where He is the One Mediator, fully God, fully man, in whose Person is effected the reconciliation between God and mankind. He will return in power and glory to judge the world and to consummate His redemptive mission. He now dwells in all believers as the living and ever-present Lord.

(Genesis 18:1; Psalms 2:7; 110:1; Isaiah 7:14; 53; Matthew 1:18-23; 3:17; 8:29; 11:27; 14:33; 16:16,27; 17:5; 27; 28:1-6,19; Mark 1:1; 3:11; Luke 1:35; 4:41; 22:70; 24:46; John 1:1-18,29; 10:30,38; 11:25-27; 12:44-50; 14:7-11; 16:15-16,28; 17:1-5, 21-22; 20:1-20,28; Acts 1:9; 2:22-24; 7:55-56; 9:4-5,20; Romans 1:3-4; 3:23-26; 5:6-21; 8:1-3,34; 10:4; 1 Corinthians 1:30; 2:2; 8:6; 15:1-8,24-28; 2 Corinthians 5:19-21; 8:9; Galatians 4:4-5; Ephesians 1:20; 3:11; 4:7-10; Philippians 2:5-11; Colossians 1:13-22; 2:9; 1 Thessalonians 4:14-18; 1 Timothy 2:5-6; 3:16; Titus 2:13-14; Hebrews 1:1-3; 4:14-15; 7:14-28; 9:12-15,24-28; 12:2; 13:8; 1 Peter 2:21-25; 3:22; 1 John 1:7-9; 3:2; 4:14-15; 5:9; 2 John 7-9; Revelation 1:13-16; 5:9-14; 12:10-11; 13:8; 19:16)

God the Holy Spirit. The Holy Spirit is the Spirit of God, fully divine. He inspired holy men of old to write the Scriptures. Through illumination He enables mankind to understand truth. He exalts Christ. He convicts mankind of sin, of righteousness, and of judgment. He calls mankind to the Savior, and effects regeneration. At the moment of regeneration, He baptizes every believer into the Body of Christ. He cultivates Christian character, comforts believers, and bestows the spiritual gifts by which they serve God through His church. He seals the believer unto the day of final redemption. His presence in the Christian is the guarantee that God will bring the believer into the fullness of the stature of Christ. He enlightens and empowers the believer and the church in worship, evangelism, and service.

(Genesis 1:2; Judges 14:6; Job 26:13; Psalms 51:11; 139:7; Isaiah 61:1-3; Joel 2:28-32; Matthew 1:18; 3:16; 4:1; 12:28-32; 28:19; Mark 1:10,12; Luke 1:35; 4:1,18-19; 11:13; 12:12; 24:49; John 4:24; 14:16-17,26; 15:26; 16:7-14; Acts 1:8; 2:1-4,38; 4:31; 5:3; 6:3; 7:55; 8:17,39; 10:44; 13:2; 15:28; 16:6; 19:1-6; Romans 8:9-11,14-16,26-27; 1 Corinthians 2:10-14; 3:16; 12:3-11,13; Galatians 4:6; Ephesians 1:13-14; 4:30; 5:18; 1 Thessalonians 5:19; 1 Timothy 3:16; 4:1; 2 Timothy 1:14; 3:16; Hebrews 9:8,14; 2 Peter 1:21; 1 John 4:13; 5:6- 7; Revelation 1:10; 22:17)

DOCTRINE 3
We Believe in the Depravity of Mankind

Mankind is the special creation of God, made in His own image. He created them male and female as the crowning work of His creation. The gift of gender is thus part of the goodness of God's creation. In the beginning man was innocent of sin and was endowed by his Creator with freedom of choice. By his free choice, man sinned against God and brought sin into the human race. Through the temptation of Satan man transgressed the command of God, and fell from his original innocence whereby his posterity inherits a nature and an environment inclined toward sin. Therefore, as soon as people are capable of moral action, they become transgressors and are under condemnation. Only the grace of God can bring mankind into His holy fellowship and enable mankind to fulfill the creative purpose of God. The sacredness of human personality is evident in that God created mankind in His own image, and in that Christ died for mankind; therefore, every person of every race possesses full dignity and is worthy of respect and Christian love.

(Genesis 1:26-30; 2:5,7,18-22; 3; 9:6; Psalms 1; 8:3-6; 32:1-5; 51:5; Isaiah 6:5; Jeremiah 17:5; Matthew 16:26; Acts 17:26-31; Romans 1:19-32; 3:10-18,23; 5:6,12,19; 6:6; 7:14-25; 8:14-18,29; 1 Corinthians 1:21-31; 15:19,21-22; Ephesians 2:1-22; Colossians 1:21-22; 3:9-11)

DOCTRINE 4
We Believe in One Path for Salvation

Salvation involves the redemption of the whole person, and is offered freely to all who accept Jesus Christ as Lord and Savior, who by His own blood obtained eternal redemption for the believer. In its broadest sense, salvation includes regeneration, justification, sanctification, and glorification. There is no salvation apart from personal faith in Jesus Christ as Lord.

Regeneration. Regeneration, or the new birth, is a work of God's grace whereby believers become new creatures in Christ Jesus. It is a change of heart wrought by the Holy Spirit through conviction of sin, to which the sinner responds in repentance toward God and faith in the Lord Jesus Christ. Repentance and faith are inseparable experiences of grace. Repentance is a genuine turning from sin toward God. Faith is the acceptance of Jesus Christ and commitment of the entire personality to Him as Lord and Savior.

Justification. Justification is God's gracious and full acquittal upon principles of His righteousness of all sinners who repent and believe in Christ. Justification brings the believer unto a relationship of peace and favor with God.

Sanctification. Sanctification is the experience, beginning in regeneration, by which the believer is set apart to God's purposes, and is enabled to progress toward moral and spiritual maturity through the presence and power of the Holy Spirit dwelling in him. Growth in grace should continue throughout the regenerate person's life.

Glorification. Glorification is the culmination of salvation and is the final blessed and abiding state of the redeemed.

Eternal Security. Those whom God has accepted in Christ, and sanctified by His Spirit, will never fall away from the state of grace, but shall persevere to the end. Believers may fall into sin through neglect and temptation, whereby they grieve the Spirit, impair their graces and comforts, and bring reproach on the cause of Christ and temporal judgments on themselves; yet they shall be kept by the power of God through faith unto salvation.

(Genesis 3:15; Exodus 3:14-17; 6:2-8; Matthew 1:21; 4:17; 16:21-26; 27:22-28:6; Luke 1:68-69; 2:28-32; John 1:11-14,29; 3:3-21,36; 5:24; 10:9,28-29; 15:1-16; 17:17; Acts 2:21; 4:12; 15:11; 16:30-31; 17:30-31; 20:32; Romans 1:16-18; 2:4; 3:23-25; 4:3; 5:8-10; 6:1-23; 8:1-18,29-39; 10:9-10,13; 11:6; 13:11-14; 1 Corinthians 1:18,30; 6:19-20; 15:10; 2 Corinthians 5:17-20; Galatians 2:20; 3:13; 5:22-25; 6:15; Ephesians 1:7,13; 2:8-22; 4:11-16, 30; Philippians 2:12-13; Colossians 1:9-22; 3:1; 1 Thessalonians 5:23-24; 2 Timothy 1:12; Titus 2:11-14; 3:5-6; Hebrews 2:1-3; 5:8-9; 9:24-28; 11:1-12:8,14; James 2:14-26; 1 Peter 1:2-23; 1 John 1:6-2:11; Revelation 3:20; 21:1-22:5)

DOCTRINE 5
We Believe in the Church

A New Testament church of the Lord Jesus Christ is an autonomous local congregation of baptized believers, associated by covenant in the faith and fellowship of the gospel; observing the two ordinances of Christ, governed by His laws, exercising the gifts, rights, and privileges invested in them by His Word, and seeking to extend the gospel to the ends of the earth. Each congregation operates under the Lordship of Christ through democratic processes. In such a congregation, each member is responsible and accountable to Christ as Lord. Its scriptural officers are pastors and deacons. While both men and women are gifted for service in the church, the office of pastor is limited to men as qualified by Scripture. The New Testament speaks also of the church as the Body of Christ which includes all of the redeemed of all the ages, believers from every tribe, and tongue, and people, and nation.

(Matthew 16:15-19; 18:15-20; Acts 2:41-42,47; 5:11-14; 6:3-6; 13:1-3; 14:23,27; 15:1-30; 16:5; 20:28; Romans 1:7; 1 Corinthians 1:2; 3:16; 5:4-5; 7:17; 9:13-14; 12; Ephesians 1:22-23; 2:19-22; 3:8-11,21; 5:22- 32; Philippians 1:1; Colossians 1:18; 1 Timothy 2:9-14; 3:1-15; 4:14; Hebrews 11:39-40; 1 Peter 5:1-4; Revelation 2-3; 21:2-3)

Baptism and Lord's Supper. Christian baptism is the immersion of a believer in water in the name of the Father, the Son, and the Holy Spirit. It is an act of obedience symbolizing the believer's faith in a crucified, buried, and risen Savior, the believer's death to sin, the burial of the old life, and the resurrection to walk in newness of life in Christ Jesus. It is a testimony to his faith in the final resurrection of the dead. Being a church ordinance, it is prerequisite to the privileges of church membership and to the Lord's Supper. The Lord's Supper is a symbolic act of obedience whereby members of the church, through partaking of the bread and the fruit of the vine, memorialize the death of the Redeemer and anticipate His second coming.

(Matthew 3:13-17; 26:26-30; 28:19-20; Mark 1:9-11; 14:22-26; Luke 3:21-22; 22:19-20; John 3:23; Acts 2:41- 42; 8:35-39; 16:30-33; 20:7; Romans 6:3-5; 1 Corinthians 10:16, 21; 11:23-29; Colossians 2:12)

DOCTRINE 6
We Believe in the Things to Come

God, in His own time and in His own way, will bring the world to its appropriate end. According to His promise, Jesus Christ will return personally and visibly in glory to the earth; the dead will be raised; and Christ will judge all mankind in righteousness. The unrighteous will be consigned to Hell, the place of everlasting punishment. The righteous in their resurrected and glorified bodies will receive their reward and will dwell forever in Heaven with the Lord.

(Isaiah 2:4; 11:9; Matthew 16:27; 18:8-9; 19:28; 24:27,30,36,44; 25:31-46; 26:64; Mark 8:38; 9:43-48; Luke 12:40,48; 16:19-26; 17:22-37; 21:27-28; John 14:1-3; Acts 1:11; 17:31; Romans 14:10; 1 Corinthians 4:5; 15:24-28,35-58; 2 Corinthians 5:10; Philippians 3:20-21; Colossians 1:5; 3:4; 1 Thessalonians 4:14-18; 5:1.; 2 Thessalonians 1:7; 2; 1 Timothy 6:14; 2 Timothy 4:1,8; Titus 2:13; Hebrews 9:27-28; James 5:8; 2 Peter 3:7; 1 John 2:28; 3:2; Jude 14; Revelation 1:18; 3:11; 20:1-22:13)

DOCTRINE 7
We Believe in Evangelism and Missions

It is the duty and privilege of every follower of Christ and of every church of the Lord Jesus Christ to endeavor to make disciples of all nations. The new birth of mankind's spirit by God's Holy Spirit means the birth of love for others. Missionary effort on the part of all rests thus upon a spiritual necessity of the regenerate life, and is expressly and repeatedly commanded in the teachings of Christ. The Lord Jesus Christ has commanded the preaching of the gospel to all nations. It is the duty of every child of God to seek constantly to win the lost to Christ by verbal witness undergirded by a Christian lifestyle, and by other methods in harmony with the gospel of Christ.

(Genesis 12:1-3; Exodus 19:5-6; Isaiah 6:1-8; Matthew 9:37-38; 10:5-15; 13:18-30, 37-43; 16:19; 22:9-10; 24:14; 28:18-20; Luke 10:1-18; 24:46-53; John 14:11-12; 15:7-8,16; 17:15; 20:21; Acts 1:8; 2; 8:26-40; 10:42-48; 13:2-3; Romans 10:13-15; Ephesians 3:1-11; 1 Thessalonians 1:8; 2 Timothy 4:5; Hebrews 2:1-3; 11:39-12:2; 1 Peter 2:4-10; Revelation 22:17)

Printed in Great Britain
by Amazon